LOVE YOURSELF FIRST!
Boost your self-esteem in 30 Days

How to overcome Low Self-Esteem, Anxiety, Stress, Insecurity, and Self-Doubt

Marc Reklau

LOVE YOURSELF FIRST. Copyright © 2018 by Marc Reklau

All rights reserved.

Cover design by lauria

Without limiting the rights under copyright reserved above no part of this book may be reproduced in any form or by any electronic or mechanical means including information storage and retrieval systems, without permission in writing from the author. The only exception is by a reviewer, who may quote short excerpts in a review.

Disclaimer

This book is designed to provide information and motivation to our readers. It is sold with the understanding that the publisher is not engaged to render any type of psychological, legal, or any other kind of professional advice. The instructions and advice in this book are not intended as a substitute for counseling. The content of each chapter is the sole expression and opinion of its author. No warranties or guarantees are expressed or implied by the author's and publisher's choice to include any of the content in this volume. Neither the publisher nor the individual author shall be liable for any physical, psychological, emotional, financial, or commercial damages, including, but not limited to, special, incidental, consequential or other damages. Our views and rights are the same:

You must test everything for yourself according to your own situation talents and aspirations

You are responsible for your own decisions, choices, actions, and results.

Marc Reklau

Visit my website at www.marcreklau.com

"To be yourself in a world that is constantly trying to make you something else is the greatest accomplishment."

Ralph Waldo Emerson

Table of Contents

Introduction 11

Part I - You are in Control 15

   1 - Take full responsibility for your life. 15

   2 - Stop complaining 16

   3 - Take your own decisions 17

   4 - Stop gossiping 19

   5 - Honor your right decisions. 20

   6 - Believe in yourself 21

   7 - Stop blaming others for your troubles 22

   8 - Don't criticize others 23

   9 - Stop judging 24

   10 - Give up guilt 25

   11 - Don't listen to your inner critic. 27

   12 - Stop competing 29

   13 - Keep your word 30

   14 - Take action. Make it happen. 31

   15 - Stop talking, start doing 32

   16 - Stop procrastinating on your goals 33

Part II - The Inner Work 37

   1 - Know yourself 37

2 - Love yourself first 38

3 - Accept your emotions 40

4 - You are not your actions................................ 42

5 - Overcome perfectionism 43

6 - Beware of false self-esteem............................ 45

7 - Level up your self-worth................................ 46

8 - Nobody is better than you.............................. 48

9 - You are enough 49

10- Don't take criticism personally 50

11 - Don't be too hard on yourself 51

12 - Gracefully accept praise 52

13 - Watch your inner dialogue........................... 53

14 - Self-concept is destiny.................................. 55

Part III - Be Authentic 57

1 - Accept yourself as you are. Basta. 57

2 - Admit your mistakes....................................... 58

3 - Be authentic. Be you!...................................... 59

4 - Don't be a perfectionist 60

5 - Don't change just to please others!............... 61

6 - Ignore other people's opinion of you 62

7 - Stop caring about other people's opinions about you 63

8 - Stop comparing yourself to others................ 64

9 - Live your own life 66

10 - Stop running away from your problems 66

11 - Don't depend on other people's approval 68

12 - Fulfill your needs first 69

13 - Stop spending time with the wrong people 70

14 - Choose your relationships wisely 72

Part IV - Happiness is a Choice 75

1 - Become a benefit finder 75

2 - Become a receiver 76

3 - Enjoy the small things in life 78

4 - Celebrate your victories 78

5 - See the glass half full 79

6 - Be grateful for what you have 81

7 - Create a positive environment 82

8 - Create your own luck 84

9 - Be positive 86

10 - Smile a lot 88

11 - Pamper Yourself 89

12 - Create your own happiness 90

13 - Write in your journal 92

14 - Look on the bright side 93

15 - Perform one selfless act every day 95

Part V - The Power of Focus 97

   1 - Focus on what you want 97

   2 - Focus on your strengths 98

   3 - Do work you love 99

   4 - Learn and practice new skills 100

   5 - Keep improving 101

   6 - Find your purpose 102

   7 - Mistakes are inevitable. Learning is optional 104

   8 - Don't give up 104

   9 - Failure is a lie 106

   10 - Make mistakes 107

   11 - Pain is temporary, suffering is optional 109

   12 - Don't beat yourself up over your mistakes 110

   13 - Freeeeedoooom! 111

   14 - Use criticism as feedback 112

Part VI - Body & Mind 113

   1 - Take some "Me-Time." 113

   2 - Treat your body like a temple 114

   3 - Exercise for 30 minutes. At least three times a week 115

   4 - Take time off for fun 117

   5 - Spend more time with your family 118

   6 - Take a walk every day 120

   7 - The Power of Meditation 121

8 - Use affirmations 122

9 - Use the Power of Visualization 123

10 - Change your body language and image 125

11 - Turn off your TV 126

12 - Learn to say NO 128

13 - Set boundaries and thrive 129

Part VII - Be Here, Now 131

1 - Be happy now 131

2 - Be nice 132

3 - Be prepared 134

4 - Be the change 135

5 - Make a difference - The Power of One 136

6 - Forgive everyone 138

7 - Forgive yourself 139

8 - Don't take rejection personally 140

9 - Let go of the past 142

10 - Don't be jealous 143

11 - Pay attention and enjoy your life as it happens 145

12 - You are not what happened to you in your past 146

13 - Give up dwelling on the past or worrying about the future 147

14 - Show everyone kindness and respect 149

Introduction

Let's talk about a very important subject. Self-esteem.

Our self-esteem impacts all aspects of our life: our relationships with others, our level of self-confidence, our professional success, our happiness, our inner peace and the success that we aim to achieve in future. It's also the underlying cause of most psychological disorders - not only on an individual level but also on the societal level.

Over the years, I've seen people making quantum leaps and reaching their greatest goals by just making one single adjustment: Raising their self-esteem.

People with low self-esteem are highly probable to making bad decisions when choosing their partners, projects, or jobs. They are less motivated and less likely to achieve their goals, and their performance is low. If they achieve goals and success, they can't really enjoy them. Their constant need of approval makes them very dependent on other people's opinions, and they constantly feel they are victims of circumstances. They are usually very hard to themselves and don't deal well with criticism. Low self-esteem causes unhealthy anxiety, depression and many psychosomatic symptoms, including insomnia.

Of course, I'm speaking in general terms, and every person is different and has to be examined differently, but those are the characteristics that commonly show up in people with low self-esteem.

People with high self-esteem, on the other hand, have confidence in themselves. They allow themselves to make mistakes without feeling guilty. They are always looking for new ways to learn and growth opportunities. They consider themselves worthy - even when criticized - and have a positive attitude towards themselves and others. They don't feel uncomfortable admitting their mistakes, weaknesses, and vulnerability and live entirely in the present. Having healthy self-esteem basically, means to be happy with yourself and to believe that you deserve the good things life has to offer.

Knowing all the dramatic effects of low and high self-esteem, the question for every one of us becomes "how can I get from low to high, from unhealthy to healthy, how can I enhance my self-esteem?"

Unfortunately, when we look around us, we see that there is a lot of work to do in the self-esteem area. The reason is that during our childhood and youth we might have developed limiting beliefs that are rooted in our subconscious and while it's fun to blame our parents or teachers or everybody else for our low self-esteem, it doesn't really help us to overcome this problem.

We have to take responsibility and become aware that no matter what happened in our past, we are capable of rewriting our story, of building healthy self-esteem. The best is:

There are no secrets to it. It's changing the opinion that you have of yourself by modifying the beliefs you have about yourself, your life, your abilities, and your intrinsic value and the book you hold in your hands will help you with it. It will help you get rid of damaging beliefs like "I'm a helpless victim and have no power over what happens in my life," "I'm not good enough," "I don't deserve good things in my life," "There is something bad in all of us."

If you make the effort and time to work on your self-esteem, the rewards will be awesome:

Higher self-confidence, better social relationships, better work relationships and just making peace with your life are some of them. Criticism from others won't bother you anymore. You will be able to freely express your thoughts, feelings, values, and opinions because your self-worth no longer comes from the acceptance of others. You'll be better able to deal with difficulties, anxiety, depression, and the inevitable hardships that arise. You'll simply experience more happiness and enjoyment in all areas of your life.

Sounds good, right?

How to use this book

There are many ways to use this book. Read the whole book first and get used to the concepts. Some of them will be easy to accept and like, others will be more difficult to accept. Don't worry. You are not the only one this happens to.

Then, read the book a second time and start working. You can start at the beginning and do one exercise after another, or you can just do the exercises you like best, first. Work through the book at your pace and don't let the simplicity of the exercises fool you. Although many concepts and ideas are quite simple, they can improve your life significantly.

Anyways, just reading the book will not be enough. If you want to improve your self-esteem, you also have to put in some work. I promise you it will be worth it.

On a personal note: Work most on the concepts you like least. Yes, you understood right. Work most on the concepts you like least. Those your mind says "No way. That isn't true for me." Many times the things you have to learn are the ones you least want to learn, the ones you reject at first. It's a mind thing.

Let's start your journey to raise your self-esteem….Have fun!

Part I - You are in Control

1 - Take full responsibility for your life.

Read closely now my friend. This is one of the most important lessons for your self-esteem in this whole book:

When things don't work out as we want, we are often quick to blame God, the universe or other people for it. I'm sorry that I have to be the one to tell you this: There is only one person that's responsible for your life, and that is YOU! Not your boss, not your spouse, not your parents, not your friends, not your clients, not the economy, not the weather, not the president. YOU!

It's scary, but at the same time liberating. The day you stop blaming others for everything that happens in your life, everything will change. When you assume control of your life and take full responsibility for it, your relationships will improve a lot. Taking responsibility for your life is taking charge of your life. Instead of being a victim of circumstances, you obtain the power to create your own circumstances or at least the power to decide how you are going to act in the face of circumstances that life presents to you.

As a result of this, it doesn't matter anymore what happens to you in your life, but which attitude you adopt in the face of the situation. And the attitude you adopt is your choice.

If you blame your life situation on others, you're giving away your power and depend on the actions of others to improve your life - and that my friend I tell you, is not going to happen. If you take full responsibility, YOU have the power to change the things that you don't like in your life.

You are in control of your thoughts, actions, and feelings. You are in control of your words, the series you watch on TV, and the people you spend your time with. If you don't like your results, change your input - your thoughts, emotions, and expectations.

So my friend - who will you choose to be?

2 - Stop complaining

Are you complaining a lot? If yes - I urge you to stop it right now. Complaining is absolutely useless and benefits you in no way at all. If it had the smallest benefit, I would encourage you to continue complaining, but it hasn't. It's more. Most of the people you're complaining to probably don't care, and there might be some that are even happy you aren't doing well. It makes them feel better and not so miserable in their own skin.

Complaining and the self-pity that comes with it are not very attractive. So, instead of complaining about something, ask yourself how you can improve it. Not happy with your weight? Start walking half an hour a day or exercising and eating healthier. No time to follow your dreams? Get up an hour earlier and do a morning ritual. Not happy with your life? Stop blaming your parents, your boss, the government or the economy and take full responsibility.

Stop the toxic habits of complaining and blaming outside factors for not living a satisfying life right now and start living the life you want. Start making your dreams come true. It won't be easy, but it's definitely doable. Stop complaining about "the circumstances" and start creating your own circumstances. Many before you have done it, so you can too.

3 - Take your own decisions

Isn't it amazing how some people always know exactly what YOU should do in any given situation? They are always ready to give you advice even when you don't ask for it, which is probably most of the time. It gets even worse when their own lives are not coherent with their talk. For example, an obese person advising you on healthy eating, a bankrupt person advising you on finance or a person whose family life is a mess advising you on how to lead a great family life. The list goes on. The only advice I would accept from people who don't walk their talk is: "Do the opposite of what I do."

I made it a golden rule in my life to only take advice from people who have already achieved what I want. Funnily, these are the ones who don't bother you with advice, but when you ask them for it, they happily answer. They don't push their advice on you.

One thing is clear though. You have to take your own decisions. What works for other people is not guaranteed to work for you, and you might have to tweak it a little according to your personality and your habits. You have the best information on your life, and you know best what works for you.

A good example is this book you hold in your hands. A collection of a hundred things that helped people to raise their self-esteem. You have to play with it and try out how some of these 100 ways work for you, and then keep practicing the ones that work best for you. Taking two or three and practicing them regularly should already do most of the job. When you dominate them, add another two or three and so on.

The problem with other people making decisions for you is that the chances are that things will go the way they want and not the way you want - and even worse if you always let other people make decisions for you, you will never learn to take your own decisions. A good trick is to listen to other people's opinions, listening closely, and then taking your own decisions. First of all, because only you know your personal situation and secondly because you will also be the one who ultimately has to deal with the consequences - no matter who advised you in the first place. So, if you occasionally mess up - at least mess up doing it your own way and not the way other people told you to. They will have an excuse that it wasn't their fault anyway, quicker than the speed of light.

Your decisions won't always be perfect - and they don't have to be. But like I said, it's a lot better to make your own mistakes and learn from them, than to always do what other people want you to do, right? Taking your own decisions only has advantages for you!

4 - Stop gossiping

On the way to a healthier self-esteem, it's inevitable that you need to let go of the toxic habit of gossiping. While at first, it might be tempting to hear the latest rumors on somebody, you might be wondering what the person who tells you the rumors has to say about you when you are not in the room. The same thing happens when you are the one spreading the dirty little stories. Your listeners might ask themselves what you say about them behind their back.

How can you deal with gossiping when it comes up? Change the subject. Say "Oh I'd rather hear about you. What's happening in your life?" or "Sorry, but I don't like talking about people who aren't present."

Gossip and rumors are harmful and destructive. And you know how it is, sometimes we're telling someone a quite harmless story, and as it goes from one person to the other the story completely changes and can lead to huge misunderstandings

Give up gossiping and have more profound conversations. People will trust you more, and your relationships will improve. Everybody wants to be with a person of integrity.

5 - Honor your right decisions.

We are so fast to torture ourselves because of one or two things that went wrong, because of one or two bad decisions. But what about all the things we have achieved? What about all the right choices?
You know how important focus is, so instead of beating yourself up about past mistakes - which you can't change anymore no matter how much you're beating yourself up - concentrate on all your achievements and celebrate your right decisions.

What are the great things you have achieved so far in your life?

For starters, you are still alive, so you must have done something right. What else?

Did you finish high school, college? Maybe you traveled the world and have lots of great friends? Did you raise wonderful children? Yes. Overcoming major personal setbacks or a bad childhood are also great achievements that should be honored.

What challenges did you overcome? What setbacks did you bounce back from? What successes have you achieved? Now is the time to look back and celebrate them.

The more you acknowledge your past successes, the more you will boost your self-esteem. And because focus comes into the equation you will see more opportunities to celebrate.

6 - Believe in yourself

The first step in raising your self-esteem is to believe in yourself. You have to create this unshakeable belief in yourself because one thing is clear: If you don't believe in yourself, how will you expect anybody else to believe in you?

Take charge of your beliefs and your self-concept. Nobody else can do it better than you!

Start to build your belief in your worth, your talent, and your potential.

I have great news for you: Self-belief can be learned! It might take some time and some training - like everything else - but you can work on it. Albert Bandera found out that 56% of success as an athlete is determined by the athlete's levels of hope, and by how much they believe that they are going to succeed. If that works for an athlete - why shouldn't it work for YOU in your life?

How do you build belief? Repetition! Do your affirmations - even if you don't believe them in the beginning. If affirmations don't work because your inner critic is (still) too powerful, do subliminal tapes, or hypnosis, or Noah St. John's Afformations. Afformations are questions. Instead of saying "I have an unshakeable belief in myself and my abilities," which your inner critic could counter with "No, you don't, you are a loser and always will be," Noah would ask "Why do I have such an unshakeable belief in myself? Why does everything I do work out?", and…oh wow…No answer from the inner critic!!

You can also visualize yourself as a person with a great belief in themselves, or you can "fake it till you become it," which means you act, walk and talk like a person with an unshakable belief in themselves.

7 - Stop blaming others for your troubles

Stop blaming others for what you have or what you don't have, for what you feel or don't feel. Blaming others doesn't accomplish anything and annoys anyone around you in the process. Accept that you are in charge of your self-esteem. You can blame your parents, your teachers, failed relationships, the government, your ex-boss, but the only person that is responsible for building your self-esteem from today onwards, is yourself.

When you blame others for things that happen in your life, you give them the power over your life. You become a victim and only "the others" can fix the situation. They have to change (and that won't happen). That my friend is a horrible way to live. Always at the will of others.

Stop giving away your power and take responsibility for your life. Blaming others is just another way of making excuses for your sorry life. Building a successful life on excuses is impossible.

You are the only one responsible for your life choices and decisions, and most of the things that happen in your life are consequences of past actions or decisions. Take responsibility and move on. If the problem is on the outside - caused by the others - it can only be solved by the outside. In that case, you can't contribute to the solution. That's why you have to own the problem. If the solution of the problem is in your hands, that's when you can solve it. The only person that can make you happy, and the only person responsible for your success - and your self-esteem - is you.

Of course, it's great to blame our parents for all our failures and our low self-esteem. It's also easy. But it's not healthy and will keep you from improving. Will you really let what your mother, or your father, or a teacher said 20 years ago define your life today?

Please don't! Take responsibility. Forgive them. They didn't know better. And instead of saying "My low self-esteem is my mother's fault" and doing nothing, just start working on improving your self-esteem with the exercises of this book. Little by little. You'll be fine.

It will be worth it.

8 - Don't criticize others

Don't do unto others what you don't want others to do unto you. Do you like being criticized? My guess is no. (If you do, congratulations - you must have a healthy self-esteem).

Resist the temptation of criticism. It's a dangerous hobby. It can give you satisfaction, fun or even the feeling of being superior for an instance, but in the long-term, it might cost you some dear friends, and you might even create some enemies. It's one of the habits of toxic people that you don't want to have around you, which means if you criticize a lot, one day people may not want to have you around them.

It's dangerous to focus all the time on the weaknesses of others. You might get so used to that perspective that one day you even turn on yourself. Criticizing is an absolutely useless behavior. The negativity you will spread will affect your own happiness and the happiness of those around you.
Stop worrying about other people's flaws and focus on yourself. Concentrate on improving your life so much that you don't have time to criticize others and always remember one thing: Those who can, DO, those who can't, criticize.

9 - Stop judging

On your way to a happier, more fulfilling life and to building a healthy self-esteem, one toxic habit you have to leave behind is the habit of judging others. Judging goes hand in hand with the bad habits of blaming and complaining and will keep you from becoming happy and developing self-esteem.

Accept others without judging them, and without expectations. Walk a mile in their shoes before you judge them, as you want them to walk a mile in your shoes before they judge you.

Everybody you meet on your journey is fighting their own unique battle, and we have no idea what they are dealing with, just like they have no idea what you are going through.

Just stop judging and show some empathy. It's easier said than done, but there is no way around it.

Did you know that each time you're judging somebody you are actually judging yourself?

The things that bother you the most about others are actually the things that bother you the most about yourself. So, put some thought into it. Be aware of what bothers you most about others and learn from it. Does it bother you that a friend is always unpunctual? Are you punctual? Are you too punctual and it would be good to relax a bit? Once, a friend was complaining to me that his clients always cancel their sessions at the last minute. What he didn't notice was that he often canceled our meetings at the last minute.

Make a list of what bothers you the most about others and reflect on it a bit. What does it say about you?

10 - Give up guilt

Guilt is one of the most destructive emotions, and the world is full of guilt-ridden people. The worst is that it's an unnecessary feeling. A whole book could be written about the uselessness of this emotion. It wouldn't be a problem if we could feel guilty for a couple of minutes and then go on with our lives, but unfortunately, many of us live with chronic guilt. We feel guilty all the time for everything, which takes a hard hit on our self-esteem. First of all, all guilt focuses on your mistakes, instead of on all the things you're doing well, and second, the painful feeling of guilt could actually lead you to doubt yourself as a person, which is toxic for your self-esteem.

Why do we constantly feel guilty? Because we've been conditioned to feel guilty our whole life. Consciously or unconsciously, since our childhood, our family, friends, society, school, loved ones, and religion has fed our guilt and enforced it through the reward and punishment system.

As children, everybody reminded us constantly of our bad behavior and compared us to other children that were behaving so much better. Guilt was used to manipulate us. The best manipulators know that if you only make a person feel guilty enough, they can be manipulated into doing just anything to get back on good terms. Their weapons of choice were phrases like, "What will the neighbors think?" "You embarrassed us!" "You disappointed us!" "Where are your manners?" Our loved ones used the common phrase "If you would really love me you would _____," and as we learn quickly, we also used the famous "So and so's parents let him do it" on our parents.

The bad thing is that this kind of treatment over some time leads us to feel guilty, even if we didn't do anything bad. Also, for a long time, guilt has been associated with caring. If you really care you have to feel guilty, and if you don't care and don't feel guilty you are a bad person. Nothing is further off the truth.

Guilt shows up in many ways. There is parent-child guilt, child-parent guilt, guilt through love, society-inspired guilt, sexual guilt, religious guilt and the most destructive form of guilt: self-imposed guilt. The later refers to guilt that we impose on ourselves. In many cases, by feeling guilty, we try to show that we are sorry for what we did, but what we are actually doing is torturing ourselves for something we did and can't change anymore. We end up saying what people want us to say, doing what they want us to do and conform to please others which results in the need to always make a good impression.

To recap: guilt doesn't serve you at all; it just causes you real emotional damage and makes you feel despicable. Stop the guilt illusion now. It's the best thing you can do. Guilt keeps you a prisoner of your past and keeps you from acting in the present. There is a huge difference between feeling guilty and learning from your mistakes. Guilt always brings punishment, which comes in many forms including depression, feelings of inadequacy, lack of self-confidence, poor self-esteem, and the inability to love ourselves and others.

The good thing is that the more you work on your self-esteem and your authenticity and being around the right people the less guilty you will feel. Whenever you feel guilty, remind yourself that it is an unnecessary emotion, and learn from the mistake. That's it. That's all you have to do.

11 - Don't listen to your inner critic.

The worst enemy you will ever meet in your life is the one that looks you right in the face when you look into a mirror. It sits right between your ears and is also known as your brain or your mind. No one will ever pass a tougher and more severe judgment on you than YOU. To develop a healthy self-esteem, you have to tame your inner critic.

That little shitty voice that keeps pointing out your mistakes and shatters your self-esteem, thereby putting you down whenever something goes wrong. That inner voice that's always telling you things like "I should have done…" "Why didn't I…" or "what's wrong with me?" "I knew I'd fail,"

"I'm not good enough" and on and on. The worst thing is you can't run away from this voice; it's difficult to quiet it, so you have to face it head on and learn how to keep it at bay. Hear the negative self-talk, but don't buy into it. Listen more to the other inner voice, the one that always supports you, understands you, and believes in you. The one that is compassionate, kind and loving and always encourages and motivates you.

When you work on something, and suddenly you start doubting or feel your energy decreasing. When you are stuck, bored or tired of the task at hand, that's when you inner critic begins speaking to you. Listen, but don't take him or her seriously. Don't resist. Respond the negative self-talk with "So what?", "Who cares?", "Big deal!", "You bore me," "Just go away and let me do my work." Then continue what you are doing no matter what the inner critic says and keep diving in. The more aware you are of your inner critic, the less he or she can hurt you. Identify the judge. Once you identified him or her, you will also know what you have to do to get it out of your head.

The good news is that the more you work on your self-esteem with affirmations, celebrating your past successes, meditation and other techniques, the lower the voice gets. Lasting self-esteem comes from knowing yourself. Knowing who you really are and accepting it.

Don't let your inner Gremlin rob you of your intrinsic goodness, doubt your worth, or your talent. Don't let him sow doubts and chaos in your mind. Don't buy his lies that nobody loves and cares about you. You matter.

12 - Stop competing

Although it might seem like it, life is not a competition. The only person you are in competition with is the one you were yesterday, focusing on the person you want to become.

It's not about beating others; it's about being content with yourself and improving yourself continuously.

They say the world is a competitive place, but it's only to those who feel the constant need to compete. We were made to believe that competition is healthy, that competition is necessary, that competition gives us meaning, purpose, and direction. Well. They're wrong.

When you are sure of yourself, and your abilities do you feel the need to compete? Do you need to be better than anyone? Do you feel the need to compare yourself to everybody around you? Do you need the validation of others to tell you how well you are doing?

A person with high self-esteem does not feel the need to compete; they don't need to be better than anybody else, they don't need validation from the outside. They don't even need a reward for doing a good job - because they know they are doing their best and because they know it's not about the result, but about the journey.

A person of high self-esteem recognizes his or her potential for what it is and strives for excellence in their life. The only competition is with themselves. The goal is reaching greater personal growth and achieving excellence in everything they want to do.
Become that person. Stop competing.

13 - Keep your word

Keeping your word is one way to boost your self-esteem that most of the time gets totally ignored.
Every commitment you make, even those you make to other people, is ultimately a commitment to yourself. If you don't follow through with your commitments and your promises you will slowly lose trust in yourself. You pay a high psychological and emotional price whenever you lie, cheat, or are dishonest. You are sending yourself the message "my word is not worth anything. Hence, I'm not worth anything". Don't undermine your self-worth and keep your commitments.

Over-deliver on everything you do and don't make promises you can't keep.

Be there, if you say you are going to be somewhere.
Mean it, if you say you feel something.

Do what you say you're going to do.

Don't lie. If you discover that you can't, won't or don't do something tell people the truth right away.

Don't play games with people's emotions. Don't tell half-truths if you want people - and yourself - to trust you.

Be very cautious about your conversations. Are you just saying things to impress and not being authentic? When you tell the truth the message you communicate to yourself is that your words are worthy, your words are important. You matter. When we tell lies or when you are all about impressing constantly, what you are saying is - I'M NOT GOOD ENOUGH AS I AM. I need to be someone else so that the other person will like me. And our self-esteem and self-confidence takes a hit.

Instead of making promises you are not able to fulfill, promising greatness and then delivering mediocrity, do the opposite: Under-promise and over-deliver. This will boost your personal value not only in the eyes of others but also in the eyes of your toughest critic. Yourself. You will make people feel great because it seems like you are exceeding expectations and going the extra mile every single time. You'll also experience a lot less stress and be more relaxed.

14 - Take action. Make it happen.

Johann Wolfgang von Goethe already knew hundreds of years ago that "Whatever you do, or dream you can, begin it. Boldness has genius and power and magic in it."

Do you plan things and then get sad if they don't turn out as you expected? If this happens to you often, then you might be missing an essential ingredient of the formula. Dreaming about the future and planning it is great, but it's not enough. To turn your dreams into reality, you must DO.

If you want to reach your goals you have to put a lot of effort into it, and most important of all you have to take action. Just sitting on your sofa and imagining and visualizing a better life is not enough.

To take action, to make things happen is one of the secrets to success and happiness in life. Just talking about your dreams, plans, and goals is not enough. It's the results that count, and without action, there are no results.

The biggest difference between people who reach their goals and people who stay stuck is ACTION. People who reach their goals are doers who are taking action consistently. If they make a mistake they learn from it and go on; if they are rejected, they try again.

Be an action taker. If you really, really want something, chances are that you have to get out there and earn it.

15 - Stop talking, start doing

C.G. Jung said it correctly, "You are what you do, not what you say you'll do." There are too many people who want to change the world yet never picked up a pen to start writing a book or an article or did anything about it. It's a lot easier to complain about our politicians than to start pursuing a political career or become more active in politics.

Your life is in your hands, so start acting on your ideas. You don't have to go for the big challenges at once. Doing small things consistently on a daily basis can get you great results. Dare to do the things you want and you will find the power to do them. And by all means, START NOW!

Remember: Actions speak much louder than words. People who just talk about what they are going to do and don't walk their talk stay stuck. But what is even worse is that this can take a toll on their self-esteem. Every time you say something and don't do it your self-esteem suffers. There has to be a match between what we say and what we do. When we communicate but don't follow up on what we say, we are mainly communicating to ourselves: "What I say is not important. It doesn't matter".

Don't wait any longer. The right moment never comes. Just start with what you have and go one step at a time. Do as Martin Luther King, Jr. said, "Take the first step in faith. You don't have to see the whole staircase, just take the first step." Stop talking. Start doing. Now.

16 - Stop procrastinating on your goals

While some people dream of success, others wake up early and work hard for it. Many times, we have a resistance against action and change when we need those two most.

You need a bit of discipline, but the rewards of stopping to put things off are enormous.

Putting things off makes them harder and scarier. There is nothing worse and more stressful than the lingering of unfinished tasks. It's like an additional weight on your shoulder that doesn't let you enjoy what you are doing. Stop putting things off. It only causes anxiety. Most of the time you will find that the things you procrastinated can actually be done quite fast with the benefit that afterward you feel much lighter and can forget about it.

Procrastinating is avoiding something that should be done. It's putting things off hoping that they magically get better without actually doing anything about them. The problem is that most of the time things don't get better on their own; they get worse.

Many times, the cause of procrastination is fear. Fear of rejection, fear of failure, even fear of success. Another source is feeling overwhelmed.

You are procrastinating when you are…

…doing nothing instead of what you are supposed to do.

…doing something less important than what you should be doing.

…doing something more important than what we are meant to do.

The secret to getting started is simply that. Get started. Just do it. Usually, by starting you build enough momentum to keep on going. Simply concentrate on taking the first step. Start by taking one small first step. And then another. And another. These small steps will add up to results quite quickly. The only difference between people who reach their goals and people who don't, between successful and unsuccessful people is one thing: Taking action. Do it now. A year from now you will thank you for having started today.

The only difference between who you want to be and who you are now is what you do from today onwards. Your actions will take you there. It won't be easy. There will be pain, you will need willpower, dedication, patience and you'll need to make some tough decisions. You might even have to let some people go. Many times it will be easier to give up. You'll be tempted to give up many times, but remember one thing: When you reach your goal it will be worth all the sacrifice.

When you are tempted to procrastinate, ask yourself, "what price will I be paying for procrastinating this task?", "Is it worth it to be burdened by and lose my sleep over a task that I could have finished in one or two hours?"

The best time to start any task is always NOW!

Part II - The Inner Work

1 - Know yourself

Everything starts with knowing yourself. It's "the beginning of all wisdom."

The first step to start working on your self-esteem is knowing yourself. Finding out your desires, your values, your opinions about the world, the people that surround you and, above all the opinion you hold about yourself.

Most of the time, these opinions and values are influenced by our education, so it's difficult to distinguish if they are really ours, or if they have been "imposed" on us by our family, church, culture or society.

Whatever the case is, wherever they come from, without putting some work in getting to know ourselves, we won't find out. It's necessary to find our direction, our own way to follow, and lastly our purpose. Don't postpone this important work as I did for many years. Once I started knowing myself, my life improved beyond my imagination.

The following questions can help you to get to know yourself better. Answer them honestly.

What fuels you in life?
What do you desire?
Are you working on making your greatest wishes a reality?
What do you really, really like doing?
What do you not like doing?
Do you do things in your life that you don't like? Why?
What are your strengths and how can they help you overcome difficulties?
What are your weaknesses?

This is for you to do. Don't ask for other people's opinions. Don't compare yourself to others, only compare yourself to yourself and how you've improved, and ask yourself how you can keep on improving.

Take risks. Make mistakes. Start making small decisions without the help or advice of others. Start to ask yourself the "why" of things and examine certain attitudes of yours or others.

On my web page www.marcreklau.com, you can download a complete questionnaire on knowing yourself and some other worksheets.

2 - Love yourself first

Do you want to raise your self-esteem quickly? Learn to love yourself. Self-love is one of the pillars of self-esteem. When self-love grows, self-esteem does, too. The problem is that in our society, self-love has become the synonym to selfishness, arrogance, and narcissism - this is absolute garbage.

Arrogance and narcissism are not a sign of self-esteem, but a clear indicator of a lack thereof. In this chapter, we will talk about true self-love. Forget everything your parents, teachers, and priests have told you, keep an open mind and dive into this chapter of self-love.

We are told to love our neighbor as ourselves, but most of the time we love the neighbor, but we don't love ourselves. We see the good in others and fail to see it in ourselves. We neglect the most important relationship we have in our lives…The one with ourselves.

The golden rule for your self-esteem will be from here on onwards: Love yourself like you love your neighbor! Be as forgiving with yourself as you are with your neighbor. Like yourself and others will begin to like you. You cannot expect to love others if you don't love yourself first.

Accept yourself as you are and remember that you don't have to be perfect to be great.

Start spending more time with the most important person in your life – YOU. Enjoy going to the movies with the best company you can imagine: YOU! Get comfortable with spending some alone time. Find a place where you can disconnect from the speedy everyday life and where you can permit yourself to be you. Permit yourself to be human.

Recognize your value as a person. Know that you deserve respect. If you make a mistake, don't beat yourself up over it. Accept it, and promise yourself to do your best not to repeat it. That's it.

Be selfish! Not egocentric. Selfish. Only by being well within yourself can you transmit this wellness to your surrounding environment. If you feel great, everybody benefits. You'll be a better husband, wife, son, daughter, or friend, etc.

It all begins with loving yourself.

3 - Accept your emotions

You are not a slave to your emotions - even if it sometimes feels like it. You are the only one responsible for your emotions. It's not others that cause your emotions; it's YOUR reaction to what others say or do. Your emotions come from your thoughts, and you've learned by now that you can train to control your thoughts. An emotion is energy in motion, a physical reaction to a thought. If you can control your thoughts, then you are capable of controlling your emotions.

You don't need to be scared of your emotions. They are a part of you, but they are not you.

It's of utmost importance that you learn to accept your emotions and also learn that there are no "good" or "bad" emotions. Emotions are just that, and every emotion has its function: Fear protects you. Anger allows you to defend yourself, put limits on, and show others what bothers you. Sadness allows you to mourn and identify a lack. Happiness allows you to feel great, etc.

Connect to your emotions and know how to express them. Never, ever neglect or oppress them. That would only make things worse. Don't fool yourself and say "I'm happy" if you're deeply sad. Analyze where the sadness comes from and permit yourself to be human. There's nothing bad about being sad, disappointed, angry or envious every now and then, but once you notice this kind of emotions creeping up inside you, analyze where they come from.

Become an observer and watch where your emotions lead you. Watch them pass by like the clouds on a blue sky. Accept them like you accept rainy days. When you look out of the window, and it rains you accept the rain as part of the meteorological climate, right? – You know that it doesn't mean that it rains all the time. Do the same thing with anger, sadness, fear, etc. Just because they show up at one moment in time doesn't mean that they will be there forever. Writing about your emotions often will help you get them out of your system. If you are angry at someone, write them a letter or an e-mail. Don't send it though. Let it be for a day and see how you feel about that person the next day.

Learn to manage your emotions which means perceive, use, understand, and manage them. It's done as follows:

1) Perceive and express emotions and permit yourself to feel them.
2) Facilitation of feelings. Ask yourself how you can feel a different emotion.
3) Understand why the emotion is coming up. There's always a reason and an underlying belief.
4) Emotional adjustment. You know why the emotion was felt.

Managing your emotions has huge advantages: You recover better and faster from problems and setbacks. You achieve better and more consistent professional performance. You are able to prevent those tensions from building up to destroy your relationships. You govern your impulses and conflicting emotions. You stay balanced and serene even in critical moments.

4 - You are not your actions

Although others may tell you differently…you are not what you do, which means you are not your actions. Your actions may be smart or not so smart at times, but that doesn't make you a dumb person. It makes you a smart person, who has made dumb choices. It happens. Sometimes, we act impulsively without thinking of the consequences of our actions, and other times we act without knowing why we act. Nobody is perfect. Learn from it.

It's easy to judge our decisions as "wrong" after we've seen the outcome. Yes. Maybe we should have done something differently. Moreover, at the moment of taking the decision, it didn't seem so wrong. It appeared to be the best option. And it probably was, having the information you had at the time.

Your actions have nothing to do with your value as a person. Don't identify with what you do. Not making mistakes at all (apart from being impossible) doesn't make you a more valuable person, so making them does not also make you any less valuable. Even if you have acted stupid every now and then, your value as a person remains the same.

You always do your best. The best you can at that moment, based on your current level of personal growth and awareness. Your decisions and actions are always based on your level of knowledge at that moment.

You might do or say things you will regret later on, because of your current level of awareness. Whatever you do or don't do; whatever you say or don't say. It's always your best - even if your best is faulty or unwise.

Don't let unwise or false decisions and actions attack your intrinsic value as a person, just do your best to learn from your mistakes and to not repeat stupid decisions and actions in future. That's all.

5 - Overcome perfectionism

People with a low self-esteem tend to have a high level of perfectionism which is a horrible combination and a sure recipe for frustration and anxiety. Will you overcome perfectionism by raising your self-esteem? Yes, you will. Or will overcoming perfectionism raise your self-esteem? Yes, it will. It works both ways. Let's look at overcoming perfectionism.

Once again self-awareness is the key. Knowing what we want and what we don't want is the key to overcoming perfectionism. It's about accepting reality. Accept your emotions, accept that it's difficult. If something has just happened to you, you might not be able to change it, but you might well be able to change your interpretation of what has happened. It's often a matter of perspective. Is it really going to matter in ten years? In a year? Is it worth you being worried and upset?

To overcome perfectionism, you have to start focusing on effort and reward it. Reward yourself for failures, for trying again and again. I'm not kidding. By now, you already know that there is no other way to learn. Yes, failure hurts, but it hurts less every time.

Third, you overcome perfectionism by acceptance. Acceptance of the outside, as well as acceptance of yourself. Realize that you don't have to be perfect. Really. You can take my word on it. Accept "stuff" and take action, cope with things, put yourself on the line, and last but not least, accept your weak points and use them as a tool for growth. Always ask yourself: "What's the growth opportunity here?"

Do you already see that you might overcome your perfectionism by doing these things?

As always, change comes by introducing new behavior like for example putting yourself on the line more, but also by visualization of new behavior: Imagining yourself, seeing yourself and behaving like a person committed to excellence, and committed to doing their best.

If your perfectionism blocks you from writing a paper, a book or starting a project use the technique of the "first draft." Tell yourself that it's only a "rough draft," and that you will improve it later (like software companies do with their versions 1.1, 1.2, 1.5, etc.). This will take the pressure away and help you to get stuff done.

Yes. You even have my permission to distract yourself every now and then. Sometimes, it's better to distract ourselves when a negative thought comes up. Analyzing or even over analyzing is not always the solution. Go for a run, Listen to music, take a break and get back to the subject in question at a later time.

Apply the same rules to yourself that you apply to others, meaning "Do not unto yourself what you wouldn't do unto others" - or better said treat yourself as you would treat a friend in the same situation. What would you do if a friend fails terribly? Or if he or she makes a mistake? I'm sure you'd be much easier on them than you are on yourself, right? Start doing unto yourself what you would do unto others. Accept failure in yourself the same way as you would accept it in others, in people you love and, last but not least, have compassion for yourself as well, not only for others.

Next time you notice your perfectionism coming up try some of the mentioned exercises and -as always- give yourself some time. You are retraining your mind. No matter what you've been told or what you've been telling yourself: It's just a matter of practice.

6 - Beware of false self-esteem

Don't confuse having real self-esteem with the attitude and behavior of people who are narcissistic, selfish and arrogant. These are not signs of self-esteem, but rather of the lack thereof and it's called Pseudo-Self-esteem or false self-esteem. Pseudo self-esteem is only the pretense of self-belief and self-respect without the reality of it. It consists of the illusion of having the characteristics of true self-esteem more than everybody else.

But we all know it. Someone who walks into a room showing off, bragging, looking like a peacock, probably doesn't have high self-esteem. In fact, this behavior is the exact opposite of a healthy self-esteem. People with higher levels of self-esteem are mostly humble and don't need to show off constantly.

The real purpose of people with false self-esteem is to protect themselves to lessen the anxiety of "being wrong and vulnerable" and providing a false sense of security. And thus, alleviate the needs of an authentic self-esteem.

Generally, people with pseudo self-esteem value themselves - and others - by what they achieve, by results and not for what they are.

Real self-esteem is founded in reality - In actual performance, in actual success, and in actual practices. And yes - you probably saw it coming - it's the product of effort and hard work.

7 - Level up your self-worth

Look around you. What do you see? Look at your surroundings and the people around you. Think of your current life conditions: work, health, friends, and people around you. What do they look like? Are you happy with what you see? Are you satisfied with your life? If not, you can change it. I'm sorry that I have to be the one to tell you, but most of us are where we are supposed to be and not by coincidence.

Our level of self-esteem is in great part responsible for the relationships we have and the situations we encounter. This happens mostly unconsciously. So, even if consciously we think that we deserve better it's what we unconsciously believe and expect that marks our life.

This is the number one reason why people with a healthy self-esteem expect and get the respect, help, and collaboration that they deserve, while people with low self-esteem are constantly involved in uncomfortable and unpleasant situations and their goodwill sometimes even get abused by others.

So, what can you do if you have low self-esteem? Work it, work it, work it and work it even more. How? Do some of the exercises you will find in this book to raise your self-esteem. If you do, your happiness and your self-esteem will increase. When you are totally convinced that you deserve more - subconsciously and consciously, your life will change, because you will act different and do anything you can to claim what you deserve.

I've seen it dozens of times with my coaching clients. As their self-esteem rises their confidence goes up, and their salaries go up. Their relationships improve, their health improves. It's amazing! You deserve the best that life has to offer you. Work on your belief, believe it and go get it!

8 - Nobody is better than you

...and you are also not better than others. You are different. You are great, but that doesn't mean you are better than others. It doesn't mean that others can't be great, too, in their own special way. Your greatness does not take away the greatness of other people. As a matter of fact, it might even add greatness to the people around you.

We were brought up with the mentality that others who have a title, a certain social position, or more money are superior to us and we have to admire them.

I have good news for you: Times have changed. Everything is going so fast nowadays. Titles and status don't mean so much anymore. For example, there are many people with a university or even doctorate title that are jobless; on the other hand, some of the greatest companies in the world have been built by people who didn't finish college or even high school. On the one hand, people lose social positions while others move upwards. Some of the richest people in the world today like Jeff Bezos or Mark Zuckerberg were not even in business 20 years ago. They are different, but that doesn't mean they are better than you. Remember that.

True self-esteem is knowing that you are great and unique and accepting everybody else for their greatness and uniqueness. You're not better than them, but nobody is better than you either.

9 - You are enough

All the troubles of self-esteem revolve around one thing. We don't feel worthy. We don't feel worthy as human beings. We don't feel worthy of our blessings; we feel that we don't deserve the good that happens to us. And if we really feel it, it becomes a self-fulfilling prophecy, and good things stop happening to us.

For once and for all: YOU ARE ENOUGH. Period. Don't fall for the trap. You don't need special abilities, and you don't need to be more intelligent or wealthy to become worthy. You already are.

Everything you have in your life, your work, your belongings, and your house is nice and influences your lifestyle, BUT has nothing to do with your intrinsic value or importance as a person.

You don't need to do anything special to reach a higher value as a human being. You already have it. It's your birthright. Nothing you do adds or removes even the smallest particle of your value, and nobody can take it away from you… except you…By self-destroying and self-sabotaging behavior.

If you are ever in doubt of your worth and value as a person come back here and read this:

YOU ARE ENOUGH.
YOU ARE ENOUGH.
YOU ARE ENOUGH.

10- Don't take criticism personally

There is only one sure way to avoid criticism: Do nothing, say nothing, be nothing.
No matter how good you are in your line of work, doing what you do. There will always be somebody who will criticize you. The sooner you accept it, the better. And the sooner you learn to deal with it, the healthier. Some people just feed off making other people feel bad or attacking their work - or even worse - personality. I'm not saying you shouldn't listen to the feedback other people give you, but learn to distinguish between constructive and destructive criticism.

The more you argue against those poor souls, the harder they will criticize you. You can't reason with them. For them, it's a game. They are in it to hurt you. Most of the time, its people who haven't created anything, because of a lack of self-esteem, or a lack of belief in themselves. So, they chose the easy way. Criticizing others.

If you respond to them or get offended by their criticism, they have succeeded. You're taking their opinion seriously.

For me, these are toxic people, and I don't want them in my life. Feedback, yes. Destructive criticism, no thank you and see you later. You can deal with them in different ways.

One: Just ignore them and don't respond to their provocations.

Two: Comment "thank you, whatever."

Three - And this is probably the best way to shut them up - agree with them. Say "you are right, thank you." This is the best way to silence your critics. They are not expecting that! They are waiting for you to contradict them, to feel bad, to get offended. When you agree with them, they won't know how to respond.

11 - Don't be too hard on yourself

In what areas of your life are you too hard on yourself? It's easy to fall into the habit of self-criticism because of past mistakes or because things didn't work out as you wanted them to. But does it serve you? No, NADA, zip!

It's time you accept something here: You are not perfect! You never will be, and - the best thing is - YOU DON'T HAVE TO BE! So, once and for all, stop being so hard on yourself! This is one of the top reasons that prevent people from living a happy and fulfilled life.

Leave the habit of exaggerated self-criticism behind, especially in times when there are already more than enough volunteers out there who will criticize you with or without reason.

Be conscious that you are doing the best you can. Keep your self-talk positive and erase phrases like "I'm so stupid", "I'm an idiot" or "God, am I dumb," from your language and thoughts and while you are at it, get rid of other nicknames you have for yourself like stupid, fatty or ugly.

With a self-talk like this, the only thing you will achieve is to focus on your weaknesses, and you know what focus does...you will see more of it.

That doesn't mean you should not to analyze the mistakes you make. Just leave the self-punishment and self-torture out. Do you know that a lot of the misery we have in our life is because we subconsciously think we have to punish ourselves for something?

So, once and for all, instead of beating yourself up, do the following things:

1) Accept yourself as you are.
2) Forgive yourself and love yourself.
3) Take excellent care of yourself.

12 - Gracefully accept praise

Do you find it difficult to accept praise or compliment? Careful. Most of the time, it's not modesty that makes us feel uncomfortable when somebody says something nice, but our lack of security and self-esteem. If you have difficulties accepting compliments, it might be that deep down you don't feel that you deserve it.

When we were kids, most of us were taught that it's bad to praise oneself. It's bad to say "God, am I good" even when you have done a great job. It was considered as a trait of the cocky and self-conceited. As a result of this, we tend to belittle ourselves when somebody gives us a compliment or praises us.

Seriously. At this stage in our life, we should have left behind old childhood education, which for sure has also been proven wrong. It's okay to accept a compliment for a job well done. Accept it gracefully and when you are tempted to say "Oh, it wasn't a big thing," say "Thank you. I'm happy you feel that way" instead. Never disagree with someone who gives you a compliment or praises you. First of all, you are diminishing their pleasure of praising and secondly, you are practically telling them that they have bad judgment and that their compliments are worthless and that can easily be taken as an offense. Remember, there is nothing bad in admitting that you have done a great job.

13 - Watch your inner dialogue

Don't underestimate the power of your words. Watch your inner dialogue very closely. The words you use to describe your experiences will become your experiences. I'm sure you have experienced situations where spoken words have done a lot of damage to others. But that's not all. Spoken and unspoken words can also do a lot of damage to you and your self-esteem. Watch very closely how you talk to yourself, irrespective of what you think about yourself. If there is a lot of comparison, judgment, complaining, self-criticism, then there is lots of room for improvement. If you are always bashing yourself, your self-esteem will be affected in a very negative way.

Most of the time, you might not be aware of the inner dialogue that is always going on automatically, judging and evaluating everything that's going on around you. If you pay attention and make an effort to observe it, you will see how it manifests in everything that happens to you.

Yes, this little voice in your head - the one that just asked: "voice, what voice?" - Comments on everything that is going on around you. What story are you telling yourself? If you are constantly telling yourself that you are bad, not attractive enough, weak, not smart enough, lazy and powerless, then that's what your world will look like, because your self-talk becomes a self-fulfilling prophecy.

Your inner dialogue has a huge impact on your self-esteem. Be careful with how you describe yourself. You are what you tell yourself the whole day. Your inner dialogue is like the repeated suggestion of a hypnotist. On the other hand, if you say you are healthy, feeling great, and unstoppable you will also reflect that.

The way you communicate with yourself changes the way you think about yourself, which changes the way you feel about yourself, which in turn changes the way you act and this ultimately influences your results and the perception that others have of you.

For example, you go out, and it rains. If you tell yourself "Oh crap, it rained. What a horrible day" this thought will lead to frustration and anger. If on the other hand, you think "Oh well, It's raining. What are we going to do about it? At least there will be no water shortage." this thought will lead you to acceptance and tranquility.

Keep the conversation with yourself positive such as "I want to achieve success," "I want to be slim," "God, I am good," because your subconscious mind doesn't understand the little word "NO." It sees your words as IMAGES. Don't think of a pink elephant! See - I bet you just imagined a pink elephant.

And - I will repeat myself – please focus on what you want. Keep in mind that your words and especially the questions you ask yourself have a huge influence on your reality. Instead of telling yourself that something is impossible, ask yourself "How can it be done?" If you ask yourself "how" your brain will search for an answer and come up with it. You can really change your life by changing your language, talking to yourself in a positive way, and asking yourself different questions.

14 - Self-concept is destiny

Self-concept is destiny. It has a huge impact on our reality. It can influence us positively, but it can also hurt us. That's why it's so important to have a positive self-concept and a positive inner dialogue. Every day, you have the choice between telling yourself "I'm intelligent," "I'm a nice person" or "I'm worthless," "I don't deserve this," "I'm so stupid."

Your self-concept often comes from what you were told by your environment as a child, but that doesn't mean that you have to take it for granted and that you can't change it. It has a huge impact on everything you do, how you do it, and how you experience life as a whole. So, if you don't like what you are seeing start changing it by introducing new messages into your life. These new beneficial messages will replace the old ones over time.

Use positive affirmations or subliminal messages and follow up with behavior, for example, smiling in front of a mirror for 30 seconds every day, or behaving like a person with a healthy self-perception.

You derive conclusions about yourself the same way you derive conclusions about others: By looking at behavior. So, if you behave like a person with self-esteem your self-esteem rises. You start thinking of yourself "I'm coping. I must be a self-confident person" and then it becomes a self-fulfilling prophecy, and you become more self-confident.

Once you realize that you are capable of many things you start telling yourself "I can deal with this. I can handle it. I'm actually more resilient than I thought I was." Your self-esteem increases, your happiness increases, and finally, success comes. There is no other way to succeed.

Part III - Be Authentic

1 - Accept yourself as you are. Basta.

If, if, if. If I did this or that, I'd be a better person. If I didn't do that, I'd be more loved. If I were able of doing this, I would be better off.

Stop it already. All those "ifs" just keep you from feeling good about yourself right here and now and postpone you accepting yourself indefinitely. Even worse...they make you feel as if you were a useless and imperfect human being.

What a waste of energy and time. You are already the best person you can be. You don't have to change anything to feel good about yourself. You can do that right here, right now. Just do it.

That doesn't mean that you can't improve little things in your life. Continuous improvement and striving for excellence should be your goals, but you are already a perfectly worthy person.

Accept yourself as you are and continue evolving, always giving the best you can in every moment. As you evolve, you will do better and better.

2 - Admit your mistakes

For many of us, it's difficult to admit our mistakes. Instead, we waste lots of energy making up excuses and justifications to prove that we are right.

This might be rooted in the deep belief that we are inadequate and if we manage to convince ourselves and others that we don't ever make mistakes, it might make this feeling disappear. At least for a while.

Anyways, you already learned that there's nothing bad with making mistakes. Everybody makes one, once in a while. Although it might feel strange and awkward at first, make admitting your mistakes a habit. As it's not such a common trait, you will surprise people, and they might even admire you for it. Admitting a mistake and taking the consequences takes much more strength than denial. And it's much healthier. Instead of losing energy denying it, it will liberate you.

I say it once again. It's okay to make a mistake now and then. Everybody does it. It doesn't make you a bad person. Making mistakes doesn't make you useless; it simply shows that you are human. Recognizing your mistakes is a sign of strength, maturity and a healthy self-esteem.

You only have a problem if you make the same mistake over and over again. If this happens, you should look at the pattern and search for the lesson and learning experience. That's it.

3 - Be authentic. Be you!

"To be yourself in a world that is constantly trying to make you something else is the greatest accomplishment." says Ralph Waldo Emerson.

Have you ever noticed that the most successful people are the ones who are authentic? They are not playing any roles. They are who they are. What you see is what you get. They know their strengths and their weaknesses and have no problem with being vulnerable and taking responsibility for their mistakes. Neither do they care about or fear the judgment of others.

For example: If you say things or agree with other people just to please them, this might be a sign of low self-esteem. Be yourself. Say what you really think, not what you think others want to hear from you (except if you are in danger). That doesn't mean that you should say hurtful or rude things. Avoid these if you can. But be aware that your opinion is as important as anybody else's. Even if your ideas are different to those of the majority, that doesn't make them any less valid or less important and you can still stand by them.

The next time when you feel tempted to agree with somebody just to please them, don't do it. Nothing good comes from being dishonest with yourself and betraying your values and ideas. If you disagree with someone, say it. If they are your friend, they'll be able to deal with it. If they can't, you probably wouldn't have gotten far with them anyway. Don't be afraid to speak your truth.

Don't let the world tell you who you are supposed to be. Don't put a mask on, wanting to please everyone else. Don't be so keen on feedback from the people who surround you such as colleagues, friends, neighbors, etc. Stop playing roles and thinking about what others want from you, or might think of you.

Stop faking and allow yourself to be your authentic self. The rewards are awesome.

Funny enough, you will notice that the more you are yourself; the more people will be attracted to you! Try it!

4 - Don't be a perfectionist

If you are the type that needs everything to be perfect, you are doomed to encounter unhappiness. Perfectionists often do a lot of extra work because they think others can't do the tasks as well as they do them, so they don't delegate. They experience a lot of anxiety and stress because there is always a fear of failure.

Perfectionism is the enemy of creativity and often keeps us from acting, which makes it one of the primary causes of Procrastination. Perfectionists are even more afraid of failure than the rest of us. If they don't act, if they don't take decisions, they don't fail. So, in the end, they don't act and don't make decisions. Or they never cease to act, to rewrite the book or the paper, because it's not perfect yet. And so time goes by, and they don't yield any results.

Perfectionism hurts our self-esteem, because of this constant feeling of failure and lack of self-acceptance you experience. If you constantly perceive yourself as a failure, it's nearly impossible to develop a healthy self-esteem. Perfectionists are also less likely to try, and less likely to put themselves on the line, which are two of the main ingredients to personal success and happiness.

Don't get me wrong. There are places and professions where you want perfectionism - for example in an E.R. or surgery, but in many other areas, it's not necessary.

Instead of being a perfectionist, become a person committed to excellence. A person that always gives their best, but knows that perfection doesn't exist and therefore, experiences far less anxiety and frustration. While the perfectionist only experiences - at best- temporary relief, a person committed to excellence enjoys the journey of their life and experiences much higher levels of happiness. For them, it's not just about temporary relief, but about lasting satisfaction.

5 - Don't change just to please others!

Don't try to please everyone. It's simply not possible. Now and then, you will come across people that simply won't like you for any apparent reason. It happens. It's not your fault, and you're not doing anything wrong. It's just the way the world goes. Don't try to change yourself to please these persons. Its mission impossible and by trying you would lose authenticity and self-esteem.

A trick that I used to finally stop trying to please everyone was thinking that in a best-case scenario 50% of the people I meet in my life will like me just as I am and the other half will not like me no matter what I do to please them. So, when I met somebody that didn't like me instead of trying to do everything I can to please them, I just thought to myself: "Well, he or she must be of the other 50%" and didn't waste a lot of time and energy trying to convince them to like me. My life improved a lot.

Don't change the way you are so that others will like you. Simply understand that it's neither possible nor necessary. Stick with the people that like you for who you are. Wish a beautiful life to the ones who don't.

6 - Ignore other people's opinion of you

Okay. I agree the headline sounds a bit harsh and surely every once in a while, a little feedback from the outside comes in handy. You should have 2 or 3 people of confidence around you, who tell you the ugly and naked truth whenever necessary.

I'm talking about the people in your life. Those who are always quick in giving you a full character and personality and life analysis based on a very small credible foundation. These are the opinions you should ignore because many times we give a lot more importance to precisely these people's opinions about us and if they criticize us it hurts. Sometimes, it even seems like their judgments of our personality, our actions and our character are correct and more important than our own. Big mistake! How the heck are they supposed to know?

First of all, they judge us based on their value system, which probably is a lot different from our own; secondly, how can they possibly know? How can some people come up so quickly with descriptions of our character and personality, knowing so little of us, our education, and our experiences? How can they understand why we are who we are and act how we act based on so little knowledge about us? Come on! Even we don't entirely know who we are...and yet we spend 24 hours a day with ourselves.

Believe me: In most cases, the ideas these people have about you are mistaken and incomplete. Unless they are real, deeply concerned about your well-being or your life, don't give them too much attention. You will feel a lot better about yourself if you don't care so much about other people's opinions.

7 - Stop caring about other people's opinions about you

In Spain, there is a saying that goes "What Pedro says about Juan, says more about Pedro, than it says about Juan." We could transform this to "What Pedro thinks about Juan, says more about Pedro than it says about Juan."

What I want to show you is that other people's opinions about you are their problem, not yours. Yup. It's that easy. You can't please everyone so you might as well stop trying right now. The earlier you accept it, the better.

Become more authentic, become more YOU and funnily enough, you will attract better people towards you and the best is that you will know that they like you for who you really are! Those are the people that are important for your development. Let go of the ones that continuously judge and criticize you.

When you are worried about what other people might think about you always remember: they are probably equally worried about what you think about them at the same time.

The fun thing is that the more relaxed and the less worried you are about the impression you cause in others, the better it will probably be. Just relax and be yourself. It's fun. You'll see.

The benefits of not giving a %&$@ about other people's opinion is that you let go of a lot of mental and emotional stress, you'll feel a lot more freedom because you don't have to tiptoe around everybody and they won't be able to control you.

So stop caring about other people's opinion about you and focus on the most important thing: becoming the best version of you and let others do their thing.

8 - Stop comparing yourself to others

For starters, don't even fall into this useless habit. You can stop comparing yourself to others right now. It's the fast lane to unhappiness. You have to have one thing really, really clear: There will always be somebody who is better than you at something, somebody who has more money, a nicer car, a bigger office, a book that sells more, etc. Accept it and move on.

The only person you should be in competition with is the person you were yesterday. Focus on your strengths and build them. Don't envy successful people, instead learn from them and concentrate on your journey to success. Use people that have what you don't have as a source of inspiration instead of envying them.

Comparing makes no sense. You will either feel superior or inferior, and you are neither one. You are unique with your intrinsic strengths and weaknesses just like any other human being on this planet. This is neither good nor bad. It simply is.

If you really have a hard time working on this one, maybe you should get off social media for a while. Studies suggest that social media play a major part in the creation of jealousy and envy because we watch other people's highlight reel and compare it to our "behind the scenes"-movie. That just can't work.

If you go to my Facebook page, you'll see pictures of me working at the beach, having a coffee on the beach, traveling to nice places. But don't get fooled. That's only a snapshot of half an hour or an hour of my day. The other ten hours I'm locked up at home working.

Also, most of my Facebook fans surely don't know that my marriage failed on the way to success. You're getting the point, aren't you?

9 - Live your own life

"Your time is limited, so don't waste it living someone else's life. Don't be trapped by dogma - which is living with the results of other people's thinking. Don't let the noise of other's opinions drown out your own inner voice. And most important, have the courage to follow your heart and intuition. They somehow already know what you truly want to become. Everything else is secondary."

The Steve Jobs quote you just read already says it all! It's difficult to add something to his wise words. Live the life you want and not the life other people expect of you. Don't worry about what your neighbors or other people think of you, because if you care too much about what they say, there will be a moment when you don't live your own life anymore, but the life of other people.

Listen to your heart. Do the things you want to do, and not necessarily those things that everybody else does. Have the courage to be different! Paulo Coelho reminds us, "If someone isn't what others want them to be, the others become angry. Everyone seems to have a clear idea of how other people should lead their lives, but none about his or her own."

10 - Stop running away from your problems

Henry Ford found out many years ago that "most people spend more time and energy going around problems than in trying to solve them." Stop running away from your problems, because they will follow you wherever you run to, right?

Any examples needed? Let's see: if you change jobs because of problems with a colleague that you didn't face, in another job you may face the same problem with another person, right? Let's look for other patterns. You might continue to encounter the same set of problems in multiple romantic relationships until you stop and solve the recurring problems? This will go on until you learn something out of the situation and address the problem once and for all.

The best way to deal with a problem is by taking responsibility for it - instead of dancing around it and figuring on who to blame - facing it and then dealing with it. It's difficult I know, but once you solve it, you can forget it. It's very helpful to see problems as challenges, as opportunities to learn and grow. Some people even consider problems as our friends and as blessings. Isn't life about just facing one problem after another? The huge difference is how you face your problems and whether you learn from it. Once you start solving problems and learning from them, life gets much easier. Most of the time, it's a lot less painful to face the problem and solve it, than the whole process of dancing around it and avoiding it. The solution to your problems is not "out there," but within you.

And to close this chapter on a positive note, let's look back to the problems you had in your life. Didn't each one of them have something positivity? Maybe a loss in business saved you from an even bigger loss because you learned from it. Maybe you were left by your spouse, but then you met somebody even better for you.
In hard times, it can be very beneficial for you to adopt the belief that life/God/the universe only puts a problem in your way if you can solve it.

11 - Don't depend on other people's approval

If other people's approval is very important for you, you are giving them an enormous power over your life and your well-being. If you depend excessively on their opinions, you are giving them the chance to influence you and your emotions a lot. You also lose freedom. If their approval makes you feel good and happy, what happens if they disapprove of you or flat out criticize you? The worst thing is that if you want to please everybody at the end, you'll please no one. Sounds familiar?

If you need other people's approval to feel good and whole, then my friend you really have a problem. Because every time you don't get it, you will feel terrible. Most of the time, the need for approval leads to anxiety, frustration and unhappiness and even worse, it makes you more vulnerable to their criticism.

The solution: Work on your self-esteem and learn that the only approval you need is your own approval. The only person you need to compare to is the person you were yesterday and always keep striving for improvement.

Search for approval inside yourself and not in other people. This will prevent a lot of emotional trouble, frustration, and anger. Give other people's opinion the importance that it deserves. Not more. Not less. But don't let it interfere with your mood and emotional well-being.

The search for approval from other people is a massive waste of time. If you worry too much about what other people might think of you, you will lose yourself on the way.

Remember: You are in control. You only have to answer to yourself. You are good enough. Accept yourself for who you are. The more acceptance, the less need for other people's approval.

The funniest thing is the less approval you need, the more you will get. Go. Try it.

12 - Fulfill your needs first

One of the principal requisites for a healthy self-esteem is to satisfy your own needs first. This might appear selfish, but let's not forget that only when we are at our best can we be of the greatest service to others, including our friends, families, co-workers, etc.

Don't be a martyr. Many people want to convince us to do everything we can to fulfill the needs of other people, even if the cost is that we get close to nothing or even lose what we already have. A lot of people use the excuse of doing service to others so they can evade taking responsibility for changing their own lives. They say that others must come first, which is a clear sign of self-deception. What might seem noble at first sight could turn out as cowardice if we take a closer look at it. Choosing self-sacrifice means that we think other people and their needs are more important than our own. It's also a good excuse for not living our own lives because we lack the courage to do it. This is a sign of low self-esteem. Watch closely whenever you get the feeling that others deserve more than you.

An example would be somebody who chooses to sacrifice and bury themselves in a missionary project to escape their own problems because they are unable to face and eliminate them.

Nobody is more important than you. Also, nobody is less important than you. True self-esteem is accepting the importance of everybody else and then serving your needs first. Your needs are the most important for you, just like anybody else's needs are the most important for them.

If you want to change the world change yourself first. Take charge of your life. Put your needs first and stop everything else. Once your needs are fulfilled, go and teach other people how to achieve theirs.

13 - Stop spending time with the wrong people

If you want to improve your self-esteem, there is no way around watching very, very closely who you spend your time with. You need to stay away from the negativity of toxic people and bring the positivity of supporting ones into your life. Associate with people who help you with your strengths, stay away from people who belittle your accomplishments and let go of relationships that constantly hurt you.

People around you can be the springboard to motivate yourself, gain courage, and help you take the right actions, but on the other hand can also drag you down, drain your energy, and act as brakes in the achievement of your life goals. If you are around negative people all the time, they can convert you into a negative and cynical person over time.

There is really something to the saying that you are the average of the five persons you spend the most time with. Take it seriously. Science has proven over and over again that attitudes and emotions are contagious. Spend your time with people who motivate you, believe in you, and bring out the best in you. Be around people who empower you.

Some people might want to convince you to stay stuck because they don't like taking risks and are afraid of uncertainty. So, stay away from the naysayers, the blamers, and the complainers. The people who are always judging or gossiping and talking bad about everything. Don't listen to their opinions and trust your own inner voice. It will be difficult for you to get a healthy self-esteem and become successful if people around you want to convince you of the contrary.

Unfortunately, it will often be people from your inner circle. Family and friends. It's complicated, but you might seriously consider letting go of the people who put you down and damage your self-confidence and self-esteem. Even spending less time with them or taking a temporary break can improve your self-esteem a lot, thanks to the decrease of negative input.

While you are working on becoming a better person yourself, grow and develop, negative people might turn away from you, because you don't serve their purposes anymore. They need somebody who shares their negativity, and if you don't do that, they will look for somebody else. They will probably tell you that you have changed, that you are not like you used to be, and most of the time, they might even tell you that you've gone completely crazy. This might actually be a good sign. The most successful entrepreneurs have this in common.

If spending less time with them or taking a temporary break doesn't work, you seriously need to ask yourself if you should stop seeing them completely. But that's a very private decision that only you can make.

Life is too short to spend time with people who don't treat you with love and respect. Let them go and make new friends.

14 - Choose your relationships wisely

Choose your relationships wisely. Especially the romantic ones. A lot of your future success will depend on it. They say you are the average of the five people you spend the most time with. But you are an even bigger average of the one person around you the most.

Relationships are the #1 predictor of long-term happiness. The one thing that all extremely happy people have in common is good interpersonal relationships. But it also works the other way around. Being around negative people can seriously damage your self-esteem and self-confidence.

Walk away from relationships that don't nurture you anymore. Walk away from people who don't value you. Walk away from negative people. Life is too short to spend it in bad relationships with people who suck your happiness out of you. Yes. Often, it needs more courage to walk away than to stay in a bad relationship, but you can do it.

Sometimes, it's better to be alone than to be in bad company. Don't let loneliness drive you into a relationship because there is nothing worse than being lonely in a relationship. There is a high probability that your best relationship will come when you are okay with yourself. It's kind of funny. It will be when you don't need a relationship to be happy anymore, that's when you will find a great relationship. Until then, work on the relationships with yourself, be a great friend. Be with people who support you and value you. Less many times is more. Also, in the relationship and friendship department, choose quality over quantity. Have a few high-quality relationships instead of many superficial ones.

When it comes to the ONE relationship Neil Pasricha, Author of "The Happiness Equation" makes a very important point in his book. He shows us how important it is to choose a happy partner because the person you are with affects your happiness tremendously.

He invites us to examine our romantic relationships with our partner or spouse and look at how much time we are happy together, how often we are unhappy together, and how often one of us is happy, and one of us isn't. These are very important questions, and you need to be completely honest with yourself.

For example, if you are happy 80% of the time and your partner is happy 80% of the time, then you'll both be happy together 64% of the time. 64% of your time together, both of you will be smiling, loving and happy. Those are the good days. Life is fun. Life is good. It also means that you are in bad moods together 4% of your time together (20% times 20% is 4%). Those are the bad days, the challenging days, the fights, the struggles. They are part of every relationship, they are normal. They'll help you grow. This means that in 32% of your time together one of you is happy and one of you is not. That's a third of your time together. A third of your time together, one person's mood influences the other. The positive person pulls the negative person up, or the negative person pulls the positive person down. It's up for grabs.

Let's look at other numbers. The people who have lived with a not so happy partner might know this. If you are happy 80% of the time and your partner is happy 40% of the time, then you are happy together 32% of the time, unhappy together 12% of the time, but suddenly 56% of your time is up for grabs. More than half of the time you're pulling your partner up, or they are dragging you down. And you walked into this being happy 80% of the time!!! What an energy drag. It's very exhausting to cheer somebody up all the time. Finding a partner of your happiness level or higher is imperative. Is your partner adding to your happiness or draining it?

Part IV - Happiness is a Choice

1 - Become a benefit finder

According to the science of happiness positive psychology, 40% of our happiness is made up by intentional activities. This includes our mindset. It's not what happens to us that determines our life; it's what we do with what happens to us. It's the attitude we take towards what happens to us. You know by now that we have a choice. Bad things happen, but it's up to us to decide how we deal with the experience. We have the choice to be an optimist or a pessimist. A benefit-finder or a fault-finder. The decision is up to us.

The "Benefit Finder" always focuses on what works, he or she always looks on the bright side of life, they make lemonade out of lemons; they see miracles everywhere - while respecting reality.

The "Fault Finder" on the other hand, lives in a terrible reality and basically feels miserable most of the time. He or she always focuses on what doesn't work, on all the things or (even worse) the few things that are not going well. Fault finders live their life centered on their problems, constantly complaining, finding faults even in paradise. It's very dangerous to be a fault finder because it can lead to resignation. Fault finders think they are victims of circumstances. They do not recognize that their reality is what they make of it.

No matter what job they find, they always have a horrible boss. No matter what partners they have, they are always awful and inconsiderate. No matter what restaurant they go to, the service is always terrible. Or when the service is excellent, the food is horrible. There is always something wrong. They are resigned to that reality, and their existence has become a painful self-fulfilling prophecy.

But there is good news: We can learn to become "Benefit finders" by training our brains to focus on the positive, by learning to interpret things optimistically - in a positive light. Yes. Some people accept the situation and then are able to make the best of it. The mentality of the benefit finder is: "This too shall pass," "Things are going to be okay again," "Been there, done that." A Benefit finder permits himself to fail and as a result feels better, is happier on the long-term, experiences more positive moods, and is less likely to feel anxious.

A great exercise for rewiring your brain to become a Benefit-Finder is to adopt an attitude of gratitude.

2 - Become a receiver

Do you find it difficult to accept a gift? Well, this stops NOW. Become a receiver. It's very important to accept gifts and things with joy, and it's also the secret to getting more of what you want. If you get a present and you're saying "Oh, that's not necessary", you are taking away the joy of giving a gift from the other person.

Take a closer look at this behavior! Is there a hidden feeling of "I don't deserve this," or "I'm not worth it" behind the "That's not necessary?" There is no need for justification. Don't diminish the pleasure of giving for the other person. Just say "Thank you!"

I dare you to practice your "receiving skills." If somebody gives you a compliment, accept it graciously with a "Thank you." Own it. Don't return it. You may say: "Thank you! I'm happy you feel that way!" and let the other person enjoy the experience.

It will help you a lot and take your self-esteem to a whole new level if you manage to eradicate the following behaviors which are tied to a low self-esteem:

- Rejecting compliments.
- Making yourself small.
- Giving credit to others although you have earned it.

Not buying something nice because you think you don't deserve it.

Looking for the negative when someone does something good for you.

3 - Enjoy the small things in life

Don't miss out on the small pleasures of life, while you chase the big ones. Enjoy the beauty around you. Enjoy the small things. Don't postpone life until you win the lottery or retire. Do the fun things now with what you have. Live each day fully as if it were your last.
Start by being happy now. Smile as much as you can - even if you are not in the mood, because by smiling, you're sending positive signals to your brain. Fun and humor are essential for a good long life, job satisfaction, personal fulfillment, personal relationships, and life balance. So, laugh a lot and have lots of fun. Think of the reasons you have right NOW for being happy.

Do you have a great job? Do you love what you do? Do you have great kids? Do you have great parents? Are you living in a free society?

4 - Celebrate your victories

It's of utmost importance for your self-esteem that you are constantly aware of your progress. Stop every now and then. Look back on where you come from and celebrate all those little wins you had on the journey. Don't take these small victories for granted and in no way let them go unnoticed.

My clients make enormous progress because they have to continuously celebrate their small wins every week. First, it might feel stupid. That's normal. Our mind is not used to this. It's used to us beating ourselves up all the time for one mistake we made instead of celebrating the five good things we did that day. It will get better. It will learn. So, if you feel stupid, see it as a good sign and do it anyway.

Every action step completed is worth celebrating. For every exercise in this book that you complete, for every little improvement you make, reward yourself. How? You can go to the movies, or buy yourself something you always wanted. Do whatever feels good for you.

If you see significant improvement, go on a little trip. You earned it!

5 - See the glass half full

You always see more of what you focus on. Hence, the benefits of seeing the glass half full are countless. The more you focus on positive things like happiness, optimism, and gratitude, the more you will see all the positive things around you and the better you will feel. The more your brain picks up on the positive, the more you'll expect this trend to continue, and so the more optimistic you will be.

Bad things happen, but it's what you choose to focus on that ultimately creates your reality. We learned from Victor Frankl that something good could be found even in the worst circumstances. Finding the positive doesn't mean to be detached from the "real world" and ignoring the negative. Both co-exist, but you choose what enters your perception. The great thing is that once you expect positive outcomes, this makes them more possible to arise - because our beliefs and expectations turn into self-fulfilling prophecies.

You can train your brain to focus on the positives and as a result of that see more opportunities with two very easy exercises:

1) Make a daily list of all the good things that have happened to you in your job, career and life.
2) At night, remember three good things that happened to you over the course of the day and relive them in your mind.

Don't get fooled by the simplicity of these exercises. They are very powerful. I hold them largely responsible for my success, for seeing opportunities everywhere now. If you do this just FIVE MINUTES a day, you are training your brain to become better at noticing and focusing on possibilities of personal and professional growth and also on seizing them and acting on them.

By doing this exercise only for one week, you'll be happier and less depressed after 1, 3 and 6 months. Even after stopping the exercise, you'll remain significantly happier and show higher levels of optimism. You'll get better and better in scanning the world for good things and writing them down and you'll see more and more opportunities wherever you look.

The things you write down don't need to be complicated or profound - only specific. Many times it's the simple things like a child's smile, delicious food, acknowledgment at work, a moment in nature, etc. Make this a habit. Do it at the same time each day. And ensure what you need for it is easily available and convenient.

One last warning. False optimism doesn't help a lot and sooner or later even leads to disillusion, anger, and hopelessness. You need to train yourself to become a "realistic optimist." Positive thinking alone is not enough. It's only part of the formula. You also have to add optimism, passion and hard work to it.

6 - Be grateful for what you have

If you would ask me for the single most important ingredient of my success; of the ingredient that took me from jobless to bestselling author, I would answer one thing: Gratitude.

The power of gratitude is amazing. Once you start adopting an attitude of gratitude, you will notice the benefits of it in just a matter of weeks. It's scientifically proven that people who practice gratitude become happier, more optimistic, and more social. They sleep better; have fewer headaches and more energy. They are also less likely to become depressed, feel less anxiety and become more emotionally intelligent. Gratitude is also a proven antidote to envy, anger, and resentment.

Being grateful rewires your brain to see more of the positive things that are around you. You will see more opportunities, and you will see open doors for you, where before there wasn't even a door.

Make gratitude a daily habit. When you are grateful for what you have, more things that you can be grateful for will come into your life. So, be grateful for what you have and even for the things you don't have yet.

Sometimes - when you're going through a rough patch - it might be difficult to be grateful. I know. But believe me, there is always something to be grateful for like you, your body, your talents, your friends, your family, or nature. Start small. When I was jobless, I was grateful for drinking a coffee in the sun, having a good night sleep, and having friends.

Instead of starting your day by complaining about what you don't have or by dreading what is to come, start it by saying "Thank you" for what you have. Focus on everything that's going well for you.

Do these couple of exercises for three weeks and let me know what they did for you:

1) Write down three things you are grateful for every day. Feel the gratitude with all your body and soul.
2) Make a list of all the things you are grateful for in your life. My list includes places I visited, friends, experiences, even bad experiences with people, because they gave me the opportunity to learn.

7 - Create a positive environment

What you see - and also what you don't see consciously even if it's there - has a profound impact on your moods, attitudes, and behavior. Among other things you can program yourself to see yourself as someone who is very successful in life. Scientists call it priming or conditioning. This is when somebody - or yourself - consciously or subconsciously plants a seed, belief or a picture in your mind and how this then influences your behavior. You can use the power of words and the power of your beliefs to maximize your self-esteem by creating a positive environment, which brings out the best in you. Here are some examples of how to do that:

Create a special place at home or in your office where you display things and objects that remind you of your successes and motivate you. Surround yourself with awards you won, with photos of your loved ones and photos of places you love. Put your favorite objects on your office table like for example, your favorite souvenirs from your favorite vacations, or your favorite books. Listen to your favorite music as often as you can, and watch motivational videos that inspire you.

For example, if you are having a hard time or if you are jobless. Now that you know about the advantages of priming or creating a positive environment you can create one for you. Only listen to positive speeches or watch a lot of inspirational videos. Have your favorite books very close to you. Read them and look up things every now and then. Have your favorite quotes close to you (in a notebook or is a special document on your computer) and read them every day. Your favorite inspirational quotes could be quotes about how to deal with fear like for example one of my favorites "Feel the fear and do it anyway" of "The cave you fear to enter holds the treasure you seek". When you are down ir have been rejected you could read the quote "fall down seven times, get up eight times" or that every failure holds the seed of an even greater opportunity and so on. The most important thing is that you don't only read these inspirational quotes, but also ACT. You and also listen to your favorite music while working. It's an amazing energy and happiness booster and definitely works. Just have in mind: In general it's happy music = happy mood, sad music = sad mood.

Try it. This will boost your self-esteem, well-being, and performance incredibly.

8 - Create your own luck

Let's talk about luck. Are some people just lucky? Why do some of us seem to be constantly lucky while others seem to be haunted by bad luck? Can we do something about our luck, or is it just something that happens to us? But before we go on: Why am I talking about luck in a self-esteem book? Because it's impossible to build a healthy self-esteem when you think you are haunted by bad luck.

Richard Wiseman studied hundreds of people for his book "The Luck Factor" and came to the following conclusion: "In science, there is no such thing as luck. The only difference is whether or not people think they are lucky or not. Whether they expect good things or bad things happening to them."

How did he come to this conclusion? For example, in one of his countless studies, he asked the subjects to read through a newspaper and count how many photos were in it. Those who considered themselves as being lucky took mere seconds to count the photos, while the unlucky ones took an average of two minutes. How come? On the second page of the newspaper, there was a very large message that said "Stop counting. There are 43 photos in this newspaper". The answer was in plain sight, but people who considered themselves as unlucky were far more likely to miss it, while the lucky people tended to see it.

But Wiseman didn't stop there. Halfway through the newspaper, there was another message that said: "Stop counting and tell the experimenter you have seen this, and you win $250". Once again, the people who claimed to be unlucky in life looked right past this opportunity. Stuck in the negative focus, they were incapable of seeing what was clear to others and their performance and wallets suffered because of it.

In his studies, Wiseman found out that "lucky people" have a lot of characteristics in common:

1. Lucky people create, notice and act upon the chance opportunities in their life. They build strong networks and have a relaxed attitude towards life, while being open to new experiences.
2. Lucky people make successful decisions by using their intuition and gut feelings. They listen to their intuition and take steps to boost it.
3. Their expectations about the future help them fulfill their dreams and ambitions. They expect their good luck to continue and attempt to achieve their goals even if their chances of success seem slim. They persevere in the face of failure and expect their interactions with others to be lucky and successful.
4. Lucky people are able to transform their bad luck into good fortune always by seeing the positive side of their bad luck. They are convinced that any ill-fortune in their life will, in the long run, work out for the best. They never dwell on their ill fortune, but

take constructive steps to prevent more bad luck in the future

So, yes. Being lucky or unlucky is purely a matter of you expecting that good things were happening to you, and of your focus. When you are stuck in negativity, your brain is incapable of noticing opportunities. When you are positive, your brain stays open to see these chances and to seize them. Once again, it's our expectations that create our reality: If we expect a favorable result, our brain is programmed to notice the result when it actually arises.

9 - Be positive

You are not born an optimist or pessimist. It's not a matter of genes, okay. Some people are born happier and some a little unhappier, but being an optimist or a pessimist ultimately boils down to one thing: How do you interpret events?

Do you interpret an event as permanent ("Never") or as temporary (one step closer)

Do you see failure as a catastrophe and give up or do you see it an opportunity for success?

I have great news! Optimism can be learned and learning to interpret events as optimists leads to much higher success. It also strengthens your biological and psychological immune system. And last, but not least…Optimists live longer. This doesn't automatically mean that all pessimists die young because there are more things to factor into that. It also doesn't mean that all optimists live long. If you smoke 40 cigarettes a day, being an optimist might not help a lot.

Also, there is another very important thing to be careful about: False optimism sooner or later leads to disillusion, anger, and hopelessness. We need to train to become "realistic optimists." Positive thinking alone is not enough. You also have to add optimism, passion and hard work to the success formula.

Another reason is that our parents are often concerned about us, about our happiness, and about our self-esteem. They don't want us to be disappointed. They think that too high expectations will lead to disappointment, but that is totally wrong. Rather, it is false expectations that lead to disappointment.

In this case, the false expectation is that events can make us happy or unhappy. That's wrong. Science found out that there are ups & downs around a base level of well-being. These ups and downs in life are inevitable, how you deal with them is your choice. The good news is that you can take more risks. If you cope instead of avoiding issues, if you confront things, if you take risks, if you deal with things, if go out and try, your base level of happiness increases and that's what it's all about.

Be an optimist. It's healthier for you :)

10 - Smile a lot

If you don't do it already, start to smile consciously today. Look at kids, for example. It's said that 4 to 6-years old children laugh 300-400 times a day while adults only laugh 15 times. We are taking life far too seriously.

Smile! Even if you don't feel like it. Smiling improves the quality of your life, health, and relationships - and of course also your self-esteem. When you smile, serotonin and endorphins (which make you feel good) are released. Smiling also lowers blood pressure and increases clarity. It boosts the functioning of your immune system and provides a more positive outlook on life (Try being a pessimist while you smile…). When you smile, your entire body sends out the message "Life is great" to the world. You'll be perceived as more confident and more likely to be trusted. People will just feel good around you.

Science has demonstrated that laughing or smiling a lot daily improves your mental state and your creativity. So, laugh more!! I highly recommend that you watch a couple of minutes of funny YouTube videos or comedy each day and laugh until tears roll down your cheeks. Some people actually healed themselves from illnesses by watching comedy all day long! You will feel a lot better and full of energy if you start this habit - science says you will even get more productive! Just try it out.

A study by Tara Kraft and Sarah Pressman at the University of Kansas demonstrated that smiling can alter your stress response in difficult situations. The study showed that it can slow your heart rate down and decrease stress levels – even if you are not feeling happy. Smiling sends a signal to your brain that things are all right. Just try it next time you feel stressed or overwhelmed, and let me know if it works.

It's true. Sometimes, we have no reason to smile. If you think you have no reason to smile at all, hold a pen or a chopstick with your teeth. It simulates a smile and produces the same effects in your brain as a real smile would. Your brain thinks you are happy and starts releasing happiness hormones and then you become happier. Of course, it's not about faking smiles and about oppressing sadness, but these little tricks can give you an advantage on a bad day, and you might end up feeling good anyway. Just try it.

If you need even more incentives for smiling, search for the study by Wayne University on smiling which has found a link between smiling and longevity.

Keep smiling!

11 - Pamper Yourself

One simple and very effective way to raise your self-esteem is by treating yourself very, very well and being very nice to yourself. Pamper yourself. You change the way people treat you, by changing the way you treat yourself. That's a fact.

For starters, write down a list of 15 things that you can do to pamper yourself, like taking some "alone time", reading a good book, going to the movies, getting a massage, exploring nature, watching a sunrise, sitting by the water, going for a walk with your spouse, calling a friend, taking someone for lunch, listening to your favorite music, taking a bubble bath, having a spa day, going for a drink, making a movie night at home, having breakfast in the best hotel or restaurant in town and so on. Be creative.

It's really amazing. Once you start treating yourself well, these little exercises will do miracles for your self-esteem.

So - as I said - make a list of all the things you will do, and then do one of them every day, or at least every other day for the next two weeks. Reserve some time for your special moments in your schedule.

12 - Create your own happiness

Happiness is a choice, and the greatest obstacles are self-generated limitations like believing that you are unworthy of happiness.

If you don't feel worthy of happiness, then you also don't feel that you deserve the good things in life, the things that make you happy and that will be exactly what keeps you from being happy. But don't worry. You can learn to become happier.

Science confirms that happiness is a choice. It depends on our choice of what we focus on. So, choose happiness. Choose to focus on all the good things that are around you, smile a lot, be grateful for what you have, meditate for five minutes a day, and go running three times for thirty minutes per week. These are scientifically proven exercises that will make you happier.

The difference between extremely happy people and extremely unhappy people is not that one group feels sad, anxious or depressed and the other doesn't. The difference is how quickly we recover from these painful emotions. Happiness is not a thing that happens to you. It's a choice, but it requires effort. Its small habits like optimism and joy practiced over time.

Don't wait for someone else to make you happy because that could be an eternal wait.
No outside person or circumstance can make you happy. Only you can make yourself happy.

Happiness is an inside job. External circumstances are responsible for only 10% of your happiness. The other 90% is how you act in the face of these circumstances and which attitude you adopt. The scientific recipe for happiness is external circumstances 10%, genes 50% and intentional activities - that's where the learning and the exercises come in - 40%. Some people are born happier than others, but if you are born unhappier and practice the exercises, you will become happier than somebody who was born happier and doesn't do them. What both equations have in common is the low influence of outside circumstances on our happiness. We usually assume that our circumstances have a much higher impact on our happiness.

Be happy with who you are. The fun thing is that happiness is often found when you stop looking for it. Enjoy every single moment. Expect miracles and opportunities at every corner, and sooner or later you are going to run into them. Whatever you concentrate on, you will see more of. Choose to concentrate on opportunities, choose to concentrate on the good, and choose to concentrate on happiness. Create your own happiness.

13 - Write in your journal

Do you want to improve your self-esteem a lot? Start journaling. As a by-product, you will also become happier and more successful. Yes, having a journal and reflecting on your days does this kind of miracles.
Take a couple of minutes at the end of your day and take a look at what you did well, get some perspective, relive the happy moments, and write everything down in your journal.

This will give you an extra boost of happiness, motivation, and self-esteem every morning and evening. It has the positive side effect that just before sleeping, you will be concentrating your mind on positive things, which has a beneficial effect on your sleep and your subconscious mind. Your focus is on the positive things of the day and gratitude instead of the things that didn't work well, which probably would keep you awake.

Make an effort to answer the following questions each night before sleeping and write them in your journal:

- What am I grateful for? (Write 3 -5 points)
- What three things have made me happy today? What three things did I do particularly well today?
- How could I have made today even better? What is my most important goal for tomorrow?

Don't give up too fast. Your journaling will get better with practice. Write what comes to mind without thinking and don't judge it. Don't worry about your style or mistakes. Do this every day for a month and observe the changes that take place! A regular notebook or calendar should do.

Journaling improves your focus and lowers stress. Studies have found that it has countless health benefits. A study by the Department of Psychological Medicine, University of Auckland New Zealand from 2013 even found that it promotes a faster wound healing! The members of the journaling group healed over 75% faster than their non-journaling counterparts. Further research shows that journaling results in reduced absenteeism from work, quicker re-employment after a job loss, and higher GPAs for students.

Think about it. People who wrote into their journal for as little as 15 minutes a day healed their wounds faster, improved their immune system and their GPA too. If there were a pill for that, it would fly off the shelves

Writing about things puts them into perspective. It structures and organizes your thoughts and feelings. This ultimately helps you get through. You will sleep, feel and think better, and have a richer social life. All of this will strengthen your immune system, and improve your health.

14 - Look on the bright side

There is nothing either good or bad; it's our thinking that makes it so. All situations are neutral first, and then your judgment makes the situation good or bad. Experiences themselves are neutral until we start to give them meaning.

If we think a situation is bad, then it's only because we see it from that point of view. If we believe it's bad, we will find information that confirms our belief (whether it's right or not). It works in like manner the other way round. If we decide to see the situation from a positive point of view, we will search for evidence that confirms our belief. Remember: You always see more of what you focus on.

Learn to reinterpret situations. Train yourself to look for the positive side of things, and you will have a lot more possibilities to see the positive effects that lie within the experience. There is something good hidden in everything bad – although sometimes, it might take some time to discover it.

It's not what happens in your life that's important; it's how you respond to what happens to you that makes your life. Life is a chain of moments – some happy, some sad - and it depends on you to make the best of each and every one of those moments. If you look back at every negative experience in your life, I bet you will find something good in it. Always search for the good in every situation and the quality of your life will change drastically

For your self-esteem, having a positive attitude and knowing to find the positive side of everything that happens to you is of utmost importance. By consciously choosing to concentrate on the bright side of every situation you encounter, you are choosing to take full control of your life, and you stop being a victim.

Your Attitude can change your way of seeing things dramatically and also your way of facing them. Life is made up of laughter and tears, light and shadow. You have to accept the sad moments by changing your way of looking at them. Everything that happens to you is a challenge and an opportunity at the same time.

15 - Perform one selfless act every day

If you give away kindness, it usually comes back to you, Use this in your favor. Countless studies prove that happiness and self-esteem grow when you help other people. They say spending money doesn't buy happiness, but it's now a fact that spending money on other people or experiences does make you happier. You can make the world a little bit better by being nice to a stranger every day.

Offer your seat on the train, hold the door open for someone, pay the toll for the car behind you, store away somebody's hand luggage on your next flight, gift many smiles and so on. Be creative. Remember "What goes around comes around."

If you perform a selfless act every day, you will notice after a while that people will perform selfless acts for you. The difficult part is: Don't expect them to. Do good to other people without expecting anything in return.

Acknowledge people sincerely, treat people nice, say thank you genuinely. Once you get into the habit of performing selfless acts, doing good will start to become the same thing as feeling good.

Improving the world starts with you. Start today, and do at least ONE random act of kindness every day. Impact the lives of other people positively and significantly, and your self-esteem will skyrocket.

Part V - The Power of Focus

1 - Focus on what you want

What you are focusing on expands. The number one reason why people are not getting what they want is that they don't even know what they want. The number two reason is that while they are telling themselves what they want, they are concentrating on what they don't want.

Remember to focus on what you want from now on. If you focus on the strengths of a person you meet, you will see more of them, and if you focus on their weaknesses, you will see those all over the place. Careful here: The same goes for YOUR strengths and weaknesses.

Where is your focus? On the positive or the negative? On the past or the present? Do you focus on problems or solutions? This is crucial. Here is where the law of attraction goes wrong for most people, and they give up. They say "I'm attracting money," "I'm prosperous," but at the same time they focus most of their time on the bills they have to pay, on the money that goes out, on the fact that they are not earning too much. So, what happens? They attract more of the things they don't want.

You will attract more of what you focus on. Your energy will flow into the direction of your focus, and your focus determines your overall perception of the world. Focus on opportunities, and you will see more opportunities! Focus on success and success will come to you. Focus on raising your self-esteem, and your self-esteem will increase.

2 - Focus on your strengths

If you often around toxic people, they might be tempted to call out your weaknesses. Ignore them. While it's good to be aware of our weaknesses - we know them, we don't need anybody always reminding us - it's even better for us to become aware and concentrate on our strengths. Why? Because we see more of what we focus on. What do you see more of? Right, I thought so. Your STRENGTHS.

So, let's look at them. Time to find out what you are good at, right? Why don't you take out a separate piece of paper, or you can even write it on this page - if there is room. Ready. Ok. Here it comes.

What are your TOP FIVE Personal Qualities and Professional Strengths meaning what are your unique strengths? What are you most proud of? What do you do best?

What are your most significant personal and professional accomplishments? What are you most pleased about and proud of having accomplished?

What are your personal and professional assets? Who do you know? What do you know? What gifts do you have? What makes you unique and powerful?

Ready? How does it feel? Have you found your strengths? Yes? Then it's time to strengthen them. Practice them and focus on them - the ones you have and the ones you want.

3 - Do work you love

You spend most of your time at work, and the 2013 Gallup "The State of the American Workplace report" states that most people are unhappy at their job. To be exact, 70% of people are unhappy at work.

If you are one of them, it's normal that you don't get out of bed in the morning, push the snooze button on your alarm clock multiple times and get up as late as possible. Then once at your workplace time seems to go slow and it's tough to face your daily tasks. So, what do we do? We make up excuses telling ourselves that we are fine and that we would probably be worse off somewhere else. We look forward to our paycheck, the weekend, the next public holiday or our vacations.

Having arrived at this point, there are three options:
1. Stay at your work and become even more bitter, miserable and unhappy.
2. Change jobs. There is no sense wasting your life in a situation like that. Maybe you can't change right now because you have a family, a mortgage, and bills to pay, but you can start making plans and looking for alternatives. Decide what you want. Set realistic

goals, divide them into smaller tasks and start working towards them, one step at a time. Do more of what you love. A career coach can be of great help.
3. Find meaning at your work and choose to see it from a different perspective. The good thing is: It doesn't actually depend so much on the work you do, but even more on YOUR perception of the work. There will always be positive components of a job, but people who burn out don't see them. Once more, the choice is yours to make.

If you love your work, everybody wins. If you're enjoying what you do, you are happier, and as a result it is much more effective and productive at your work, boosting the companies result, adding to the happiness of everyone around you, providing your clients with a great product and great customer service. As I said: Everybody wins.

4 - Learn and practice new skills

Learn something new at least once a month. Do different activities that will put you in touch with your abilities. It doesn't have to be a massive project. Just a small thing. One word of a new language every day, control your budget, learn a new cooking recipe. By learning new things, you will gain confidence in yourself.

Once you have learned new skills, you can put it in practice when the occasion arises. What does this have to do with your self-esteem? A lot! First of all, you're taking life in your hands and not depending on other people. Second: acquiring new skills, things that maybe you thought you weren't able to do before, and putting them into practice will strengthen your feelings of capability, competence, and self-worth, which are extremely important ingredients of your self-esteem. Once they go up, your self-esteem goes up. They will also contribute directly to your feeling of being in control of your life, which is another crucial ingredient of self-esteem. The more things you learn, the more you'll be in control and not have to depend on other people.

Another side effect is that small things often lead to big results. In a study of the luckiest people, it was found out that they do new things every day. These small changes lead to change and "chance opportunities." Try it.

5 - Keep improving

See yourself as a work in progress. You never stop learning. Make an effort at improving yourself. A good way to improve your self-esteem is by working on your strengths and improving your weaknesses. It all starts once again with looking into ourselves, asking ourselves what we would like to change about ourselves, or what we would like to achieve.

Then it's time for setting goals. Realistic goals. They should stretch you a little bit though.

If you are not the self-punishing type, you can set huge goals. If you reach them, great. If not - also great. You celebrate how far you have come and then keep going after your goal. If you are more of the self-torture type when you don't reach a goal, then it's better to set smaller goals. Once you set your goals, make a plan on how to get there and keep track of your progress.

A nice side effect is that the will to keep improving, the will to keep learning, the habit of always asking questions is also one of the two characteristics that distinguish extraordinarily successful people from the rest. The other one is believing in yourself.

Keep improving. The reward is marvelous!

6 - Find your purpose

Mark Twain once said that, "the two most important days in your life are the day you are born, and the day you find out why." Man, was he right.

What is your purpose? Why are you here? What would you do if success was guaranteed? What would you do if you had ten million dollars, seven houses, and have traveled to all of your favorite destinations? Answering these questions will lead you to your purpose.

If you feel like you are driving without a roadmap or a GPS and don't really know where to go, or if you never quite know what you are doing here and why, and you feel kind of lost and empty, then that's a sign that you have not found your purpose yet. I bet you already know your purpose, it has crossed your mind every now and then, but you said "no way, who am I to ...."

You are not alone. The lack of purpose seems to have become a mass epidemic in our time. I've been there, too. Don't worry. It can be fixed. Let's work on it.

You can find clues to your purpose by examining your values, skills, passions, and ambitions, and by taking a look at what you are good at. Have the courage to answer the following answers about yourself and write them down. They will lead you to your purpose. Be honest with yourself. Nobody else, but you, can see the answers. Don't skip them. Once you answer these questions honestly, everything will change.

Who am I?
Why am I here?
What inspires me?
Why do I exist?
What do I really, really, really want to do with my life?
When do I feel fully alive?
What am I doing when time flies by?
What are my greatest strengths?
What would I do if success was guaranteed?
What would I do if I had ten million Dollars, seven houses, and had traveled all around the world?

No worries. No pressure. You don't have to rush into something new, but you can start doing more of the things you love. When you find your purpose, things will start to fall into place, and incredible things will start to happen. You will start to attract people, opportunities, and resources naturally. Nothing attracts success more than somebody who is doing what they love to do.

7 - Mistakes are inevitable. Learning is optional

Do you want to know the secret that will lead you to not make one single mistake in your life anymore? Me, too! Unfortunately, this secret doesn't exist.

Mistakes are inevitable, and you will do good to accept that you will make one every now and then on the journey of your life. Some small and some big ones. Some will even make you feel miserable. But even then in our darkest hours, we have to remember that mistakes are very important for our personal growth and we can learn from every single one of them.

If we do, our mistakes can be an invaluable source for our development. Every time you make a mistake, you are eliminating one wrong solution, and you are taking one step forward in finding the correct one, like Thomas Edison who found 10,000 ways of how the light bulb doesn't work and Babe Ruth whom every strike brought closer to his next home run.

Allow yourself to make mistakes, to err, to slip up and you will be rewarded with improvement opportunities on all levels, which will considerably increase your chances of reaching your goals, success, and well-being.

8 - Don't give up

On the journey to a healthy self-esteem, obstacles might show up. More than once you will be tempted to give up and go back to your old ways. Don't!

I know I might be repeating myself. It's just so important that you keep on believing in yourself and working even in the face of resistance. And resistance will show up. Many times, life gets the messiest before the big breakthrough. As if life, God, the universe, or your mind wanted to test you one last time and see if you are really serious about your goal. Often, my coaching clients had "the worst week ever" just before the following week of getting a new customer, a raise, a job, a huge breakthrough, etc.

Very often, when everything seems to go against you, when doubts and fear are doing the best to make you quit, when you are close to giving up, it's when you are closer to victory than you've ever dreamt of. So, when facing a situation like this, just push towards your goal a little more. It's this last push that can make a difference between "failure" and success.

Do you know the story of the man who searched for gold, digging 10 meters deep and then gave up? The next guy who came to the mine dug just half a meter deeper and found a massive gold deposit. There are hundreds of stories like this. Don't be the person who gives up just before hitting the jackpot.

Thomas Alva Edison, one of the greatest inventors in American history, brings us his surefire way to success: "The most certain way to succeed is always to try just one more time." When you are close to giving up think of his words and of the words of Mary Anne Radmacher, who teaches us that: "Courage doesn't always roar. Sometimes courage is the quiet voice at the end of the day saying, "I will try again tomorrow."

Don't give up.

9 - Failure is a lie

How did you learn to walk? How did you learn to eat? How did you learn to draw?

By trying over and over again. By falling over and over again. Could you have learned walking without falling hundreds of times? I doubt it. Remember how you ate when you were a toddler? It took some practice to eat as you eat today.

As kids, we know it. We enjoy the joy of learning. We enjoy falling and getting up again. And then, when you get to a certain age and notice that people are watching you, it goes away... Suddenly, you want to maintain a certain image. Suddenly, you start avoiding instead of trying it. The famous "what if" comes in. "What if I fall?", "What if she says no?", "What if my classmates don't like what I say?" And we pay the price for it. This issue of not coping affects our self-esteem, it affects our confidence, it affects our resilience, and it affects our happiness levels in the long-term.

Remember how you learned! You fall, and then you get up again. You miss and then you hit. There is no other way. There is no other way to grow. There is no other way to learn. There is no other way to become resilient, to become happier, and to become more successful. It's trying and failing, trying and failing and succeeding and trying and failing again. Accepting your mistakes as feedback and learning from them.

As Harvard Professor Tal Ben Shahar says: "Learn to fail or fail to learn."

You MUST accept that you will fail every now and then. I hope you fail many times! Don't misunderstand me now. It's because the more often you fail, the more often you will succeed. It's a numbers game. Babe Ruth one of the best baseball players in history said: "Every strike brings me closer to the next home run."

10 - Make mistakes

This chapter is about having a different approach toward the journey of your life, toward each step of the way, and especially towards making mistakes. Do you know that the biggest mistake you can make is being afraid of making one?

I have to warn you. Even after this chapter, you will not be able to skip the pain of failure, because it's inevitable. I hope for you, though, that you will acquire a more rational, more helpful, and more empowering approach towards making mistakes.

Remember that every time you fail, every time you make a mistake you are learning something that is necessary for your personal growth and that provides you with information and motivation. Every mistake you make - if you learn from it - can become another stepping stone to your success. Mistakes are only a problem if you don't learn from them. Stop punishing yourself for making mistakes. Don't torture yourself; don't tell yourself you are stupid. Learn something from it and move on. Avoid the mistake of believing that you always make the wrong decisions. This will only make you feel insecure and raise the possibility to make new mistakes.

Instead, be nice to yourself when you make a mistake. It happens. Learn the lesson and avoid making the same mistake in the future. That's it. Easy, isn't it? Be prepared to make mistakes. Be prepared for the worst-case scenario. "What happens if...?" So in the worst case, you make a mistake. What happens? You learn. It's not comfortable. It hurts, but you will bounce back again - as you did before. That's it.

Let me finish this chapter with a story - some attribute it to IBM, some attribute it to Southwest airlines – a case where an employee made a strategic error. He lost the company a million dollars. So, the next day he goes to see his boss and hands him his letter of resignation. The boss asks "Why?" The employee answers: "I just made a mistake that cost the company a million dollars" And his boss answers: "No way. I will not accept your resignation. I just invested a million dollars in your education!"

Make the best of what happens to you. See every mistake as a learning opportunity, a learning experience, or a stepping stone.

11 - Pain is temporary, suffering is optional.

Let's be honest. Sooner or later, bad things happen to good people. This is part of the journey. We have to accept it. Even the happiest people in the world experience negative emotions like sadness, anger or disappointment. But you have a choice: You can see the bad experience purely as that: As something horrible, a catastrophe and suffer, or you can look for the lesson this hardship contains, use it for your personal development and make the best out of it.

You can use the sad moments in your life to teach yourself to enjoy the happy moments even more and to be more grateful for everything you have in life.

Overcoming hardship can even strengthen your self-esteem and self-confidence and the next time a bad experience comes around, you already know you can bounce back and come back stronger than ever before because you've done it before. If you learn the right lesson, hardship can make you a more humble, patient, empathic, resilient, and even happier person. Many times, the happiest persons have had the saddest personal stories in their life.

History is full of people who had terrible things happen to them and then made the best out of the experience and left their mark on humanity. The Jewish Psychologist Victor Frankl taught us the ultimate freedom based on his horrific experiences in a German concentration camp: "to choose one's attitude in any given set of circumstances, to choose one's own way." When life throws you a curveball remember that pain is inevitable, but suffering is optional.

12 - Don't beat yourself up over your mistakes.

Why are our mistakes hurting us so much? Why are we blaming ourselves for our mistakes all the time? Why do we actually beat ourselves up over mistakes that were impossible to foresee? Why do we feel guilty for problems we couldn't possibly do anything about? Why?

Don't engage in this kind of self-destroying and self-weakening behavior. This is poison for your self-esteem.

We already concluded that mistakes are inevitable. Once you make a mistake, there is absolutely no use in beating yourself up about it. You can't change it anyway.

Simply learn from that mistake. Once you start learning from your mistakes, there is no more sense in beating yourself up about it.

When I make a mistake or a wrong decision - and that happens a lot - instead of beating myself up and getting all negative, I always think to myself that given the circumstances and given the information I had at the time; it was the only and best decision I could take at that moment. It's always easy to judge our decisions looking back and having all the information, but most of the time we just don't have all the information when we have to take the decision.

This technique helps me to come to terms with myself and helps me to learn. Try it and see how it will work for you.

13 - Freeeeedooooom!

Many of us on our journey give far too much importance to other people's opinions. Two of the worst questions that we carry around with us - probably coming from our parents, education, and society - are: "What will other people think of us? Or "what will other people say."

Honestly. What would your life be without these questions? It would probably be a lot better. I've met countless people who entered into bad relationships, or jobs or stayed in bad relationships and bad jobs just because of these questions.

And what happens? If we care too much about what other people think of us, we will start living the life other people want for us and not the life we want for ourselves. We do what they want, instead of what we want; we constantly do things to get the confirmation of others, not because we like doing it.

The more important other people's opinions become for us, the more of our freedom we give away; and the less we live life the way we want. We do less of what we want to do, we say less of what we want to say, and we even think less of what we want to think and we inevitably pay the price for it. It's impossible to develop a healthy self-esteem while we overrate the opinion of others and take them to heart. Even worse our self-esteem gets worse because in the worst case we feel we are lesser persons than those whose opinions we depend on. It's of utmost importance to (re-) claim your freedom and be independent from other people's opinion. It's a great life. You will love it.

14 - Use criticism as feedback

Remember the chapter about criticism and how not to take them personally? Now that it's said, there's more to it. There are few things that tell you more about your self-esteem than your reactions towards criticism. Did you ever notice that when you are super happy with yourself, other people's critics rarely affect you? On the other hand, when our self-esteem is a little low, we are more likely to be sensitive towards critical comments and see other people's criticism as a personal attack.

Let's face it. Criticism - even if they are constructive - hurt a little. And that's ok. When I'm starting a book, I'm very sensitive to criticism. I only give sample chapters away to people who I know will give me good feedback, because in the beginning stages of a new book I don't have sufficient confidence. Later on, I'm more open to it, and now I use the criticism to make my next books better.

So, when confronted with honest, constructive criticism use it as feedback and learn from it. Also, remember that if someone criticizes something you do, that doesn't mean that they criticize you as a person. If somebody makes negative comments just to attack you personally, take the comments with a smile - the best way to show a critic your teeth is to smile -, go to chapter "Don't take criticism personally" and read it once again.

Part VI - Body & Mind

1 - Take some "Me-Time."

Alone time is important. Make it a habit of taking at least half an hour every day for yourself. This is YOUR time, and you can do whatever you like with it. It's a good time to write into your journal, plan your day, read or meditate. I would recommend you to do a morning ritual. Studying the most successful people, I found out that most of them have a morning routine and do exactly those things.

Your morning ritual could look like this:
Get up at 5.30AM
Walk or run for 20 minutes
Gratitude for 5 minutes
Meditate for 5 minutes
Read for 20 minutes
Write into your journal for 5 minutes

This ritual will change your life and take it to the next level regarding self-esteem, but also happiness and success. At the end of the book, you will find a bonus chapter from my book "30 Days - change your habits, change your life" that describes it in more detail.

We usually don't take enough care of ourselves because we are always so busy taking care of everybody else: our jobs, our families, our friends. And while that is very nice for the others, it's also a huge mistake. To maintain a healthy self-esteem, it's important to take excellent care of ourselves and to remember that we also have needs and wishes that need to be taken care of. It's an absolute must to take a "me-time" every single day.

2 - Treat your body like a temple

Isn't it ironic? If you ask people what is the most important thing in their life the answer, mostly, will be "my health"; nevertheless, many people drink alcohol, smoke, eat junk food, or even take drugs, and spend most of their free time on the couch without any physical activity.

A healthier life is only a decision away. Decide NOW to live healthier. Follow a balanced diet, exercise regularly, and stay or get in physical shape so that your brain has all the nutrition it needs to produce a positive lifestyle.

Take care of your body, because if the body is not well, the mind doesn't work well either. Here are some examples:

Eat more fruit and vegetables.
Reduce your intake of red meat.
Drink at least 2 liters of water each day. Eat less!
Stop eating junk food.
Get up early.
Get enough sleep.
Exercise at least three times a week.

Treat your body like a temple, and your body will compensate you with a long, healthy life. A great side-effect of a healthy, disciplined life is that it will automatically raise your self-esteem.

3 - Exercise for 30 minutes. At least three times a week

The benefits of exercising at least every other day are countless:
- Your self-esteem increases and you experience less stress and anxiety.
- Your mood gets boosted, and your work performance enhances.
- Your sleep quality improves.
- You feel better and have a lot of energy.
- Weight loss.
- Your health improves: People who exercise are much less prone to physical diseases.

The likelihood of diabetes, osteoporosis, heart failure, high cholesterol, and even certain kinds of cancer are reduced significantly, and the immune system gets strengthened.

After you go for a run, your brain is most susceptible to creating new neural pathways

Your memory improves, meaning that you retain material you have learned much better You become much more creative

The most incredible research about the positive benefits of exercise was done by Michael Babyak from Duke Medical

School: He took 156 patients with major depression - people in very bad shape - showing a number of symptoms like insomnia, eating disorders, lack of desire to act, depressed mood, many of them suicidal with attempts or thoughts about suicide and divided them into three groups.

The first group did 3 x 30 minutes of exercise of moderate difficulty (jogging, swimming. race walking). The second group was put on medication (Zoloft), and the third group was on medication and exercise. After four months Babyak got some stunning results: 60% of the subjects were not experiencing the major symptoms of depression anymore, meaning they recovered! All groups experienced similar improvements in happiness which means that exercise proved just as helpful as antidepressants!!! The medication group took about 10-14 days to get over depression, while the exercise group took close to a month - but later there was no difference. Amazing isn't it? But there is more:

Six months after the study ended, when the participants were no longer given the medication or no longer pushed to exercise, they had a look at the relapse rate. Out of the 60% that got better 38 percent of our "only medication" group went back and had major depression again. From the third group (medication & exercise) it was 31%. But from the exercise group, there were only 9% who fell back into depression.

This means that exercise is not only a very powerful, but also a lasting mood lifter. Careful now. I'm not saying that medication isn't necessary anymore, but that perhaps we should first ask whether exercise or the lack thereof is the underlying reason for the experience.

Some people even say that exercise is like taking an anti-depressant!
If I didn't convince you by now:

You will also have better sex. Both men and women. Exercise strengthens libido and enhances the likelihood of orgasms. People, who exercise more, regularly have more and better sex.

Before you start your exercise program, remember: Recovery is very important and more is not always better. Funny enough, the symptoms of overtraining are very similar to the symptoms of under training. Also, don't force yourself to exercise. Do activities that you enjoy doing such as swimming, for example. Even walking an hour a day can make a huge difference.

4 - Take time off for fun

With the stressful, fast-paced life that we are living, it has become even more important to slow down our pace of life and take a break. There is much more to life than only increasing its speed. Instead, take some time off. Recharge your batteries by being around nature. You can start by scheduling some relaxation time into your weekly schedule. If you dare - start with weekends in which you are completely disconnected from the Internet, TV, and your electronic games.

Take time off and connect with nature. It doesn't have to be a long trip. Walk in the woods, on the beach, or in a park whenever you get the chance and observe how you feel afterward. Or just lie down on a bench or in the grass and contemplate the blue sky. When was the last time you walked barefoot on grass or on beach sand?

The latest research found out that spending time outside boosts your mood, broadens your thinking, and improves your working memory. But not only that. One study found out that participants were substantially happier outdoors in all natural environments than in urban environments.

One key element you should always make time for is to spend more time with friends and family. Not staying in touch with friends and spending too much time at work are two of the top five regrets of the dying. Science found that one factor that extremely happy people have in common and which differentiates them from everybody else is the strength of their social relationships. Time spent with family and friends makes a huge difference in our happiness.

Take time off for your hobbies, doing activities that challenge you, spending time with your family and friends, reading, or volunteering. In contrary to common thinking, taking time off for doing fun stuff doesn't make you less, but more productive.

5 - Spend more time with your family

In case I didn't make it clear in the last chapter and just to make sure that you won't skip it, I will mention it once more. Don't neglect your family because of your work. And you don't have to take my word for it. It's reported that one of the biggest regrets of people on their death-bed is having spent too much time at the office and not enough time with their loved ones. But there is more. The strength of your social relations is also the number one predictor of your future happiness.

Are you one of the leaders and executives who spend too much time at work and no time with your family? And you are probably justifying yourself by saying that you are doing this for your family?

Do you see that it's kind of absurd? You are not spending time with your family, but you're doing it for your family? When will you spend time with your family? When you retire? Maybe then your family won't want to spend time with you anymore…

Start making time for your family NOW! It's possible. If you want to make the time, you'll find the time. It's all about your priorities. It's about your values. Family is the most important thing in your life, and if it isn't for you, it will be difficult to make time. Do the best you can. And if you are with the family do yourself and them a favor and be FULLY PRESENT. That means no work calls, no work e-mails. If you don't have a lot of time, then make the time you spend with your loved ones quality time. One hour of quality time can be worth more than five hours of you being only half present or thinking of work all the time.

WAKE UP! Value your family and friends. They are your constant source of love and mutual support, which increases your self-esteem and boosts your self-confidence.

As I said before: The latest science confirms that spending time with your loved ones will not damage your productivity. On the contrary, it will make you even more productive.

At least try it out for a while.

6 - Take a walk every day.

Go out and spend time in nature and connect with it whenever possible. Go for a run or a walk in the morning hours, and it will energize you for the whole day. Take the time and walk through the woods or on the beach to disconnect from the fast and stressful rhythm of the lives we lead. Watch a sunset or a sunrise. Listening to the silence and peace will help you to relax. Taking a walk will reenergize your body, mind, and soul.

There is a Stanford study which concludes that walking improves your creative thinking. Another study showed that walking half an hour a day - every day - is just as good as exercising.

Walking 30 minutes a day will - among other benefits - decrease your cholesterol, improve your performance, lower your stress levels, improve your immune system, eliminate fat, and improve your mood. It might even shield you against burnout, and you can analyze your emotions while you're walking. Last but not least, you will fall asleep easier and have a better and more refreshing sleep at night. When will you start walking one hour per day? Do it for 30 days and let me know how it feels! You might feel a lot better after only a week.

7 - The Power of Meditation

Meditation has gone mainstream. Maybe you've already experimented with it. If not, I highly recommend it to you. It's easier than you think. And in its easiest form, you basically can't do anything wrong. There are various kinds of meditation like Yoga, focusing on your breath, praying, sitting meditation, Tai Chi and so on. All meditations have some things in common, like focusing on one thing, for example, movement, posture, breath, or a flame and deep-breathing. Meditating rewires your brain for happiness. It improves your focus and clarity. It calms the mind after a stressful day and works against anxiety, anger, insecurity, and even depression.

Meditation is a great and easy way of getting rid of stress and quieting our information-overloaded mind.

Other studies point out that meditation can reduce blood pressure and pain response. Just sitting still for 15 to 20 minutes, once a day can really make a difference and help you to recharge. If you do it twice a day...even better!

When will you begin your habit of daily meditation? What are you waiting for? Meditating for 20 minutes a day will surely provide you with great results once you have made it a habit. It will rewire you to be happier and positively impact your self-esteem. Try it out and figure out what works best for you.

8 - Use affirmations

A great way to raise your self-esteem is the use of affirmations. The regular practice of affirmations can help us to change our beliefs about life and ourselves and thereby reprogram our minds. If you have a low self-esteem, it's mostly a product of conscious or unconscious programming during your childhood by your family, friends, teachers, society, the media and even by yourself.

By repeating positive statements many times a day, you convince your subconscious mind to believe them. Once your subconscious mind is convinced, you start acting accordingly. You start believing you are a person with high self-esteem and then you become it. Yes, it really is that simple. You have to practice a lot though. Affirmations help you develop the mentality, thoughts and beliefs you need to take your self-esteem to the next level. I highly recommend writing down your affirmations and reading them out loud various times daily.

It's important to state them positively and in the present so that your subconscious mind can't differentiate between if it's already true or "only" imagined. Affirmations do have to be personal, positively stated, specific, emotionally charged, and in the present tense. Here are some examples:

I deserve to be happy and successful.
I am competent, smart and able.
Every day and in every way I'm feeling better and better
I love the person I am becoming.
I follow up with everything I say and do.

The more you practice, the better you get. The first time you say "I'm a person with healthy self-esteem and happy about it" your inner voice will still say "No, you are not. You are small, and you have no right to happiness." However, after repeating it 200 times every day for a week, you should have silenced your inner critic. Make your affirmations your permanent company. Repeat them as often as you like and have a look at what happens in your life.

Nevertheless, some studies claim that affirmations actually have negative effects for people with very low self-esteem. If your inner critic just doesn't get convinced, if you notice no benefit at all, or if things get worse instead of better - which happens in very few cases - try other techniques like subliminal tapes (they go directly to your subconscious without any chance of self-judgment) or ask yourself other questions such as "Why am I so happy? Why is everything working out?" Did you just notice? When you ask a question, the inner critic stays quiet. Instead of self-talking you down, your mind is now searching for answers to the question you asked. Noah St. John has written a whole book on the power of asking yourself the right questions. His "Book of Afformations" might be able to help you.

9 - Use the Power of Visualization

Every day, there is more scientific proof that the power of visualization really works. For example, if you look at your hand now and then close your eyes and imagine your hand thanks to MRI, scientists can see that in your brain the same thing happens. For your brain, there is no difference between the "real" hand and the imagined hand.

You can use visualization to create mental images of behavior or results that you want in your life. Done often enough, your brain will provide you with the motivation, ideas and focus needed to transform the image into reality. Yes, you can raise your self-esteem visualizing yourself having more self-esteem! Isn't that great?

There are various studies where athletes used visualization to increase their performance and get the results they wanted. Many successful personalities use visualization to reach their goals, for example, Will Smith, Jim Carrey, Oprah Winfrey, Wayne Gretzky, Jack Nicklaus, Greg Louganis, Arnold Schwarzenegger and many, many more.

How do you do it? Visualize your goals, the character trait you want or your ideal life for 5 minutes. See yourself as already having achieved your goals. See how everything comes to you effortlessly. Put a lot of emotions and all your senses into your visualization. Feel it, smell it, hear it. Visualize what you really, really want. The more vivid your visualization is, the better the impact it will have.

Optionally, you can even do a "Vision Board." A vision board could be an A3 sheet of cardboard where you put pictures of what you want, who you want to be, where you want to live etc. It's quite fun.

Now, by just writing this I think it's time for me to make another vision board. I'll go to the store and buy a couple of journals and cut out the photos that represent my goals. For example, a photo of my dream house, some dollar bills for wealth, the view of a full auditorium for speaking gigs and so on. I'll probably put it up in my bedroom. Then as a part of my morning ritual every day I will look at it for 5 minutes and visualize. And maybe, for another 5 minutes before going to bed. Why not?

If you Google "vision board", you will get over 27 million results. I'm sure you can find some inspiration. You could also make a screensaver or a presentation of various photos on your computer or desktop.

Just one more thing. Having a vision board is not enough. If you don't take action, nothing will happen. You will only reach your goals through taking action

10 - Change your body language and image

Act as if. Act as if you already have high self-esteem. Speak like a person with high self-esteem, walk like a person with high self-esteem, have the body posture of a person with high self-esteem. Your brain can't differentiate between reality and imagination; use it to your advantage. Fake it till you become it! It works.

Smile a lot. Smiling will actually make your feel better because it sends a signal to your brain that everything is great. A nice side effect is that others will feel more comfortable around you, which will add to your self-esteem. You'll think "Oh. Other people want to be around me; I must be a nice person."

Remember that when you feel sad and depressed, you usually look at the floor, keep your shoulders down, and adopt the posture of a sad person, right?

Just the fact of putting your shoulders straight and look other people straight in the eye will improve your well-being and confidence. Your body language actually influences who you are.

Amy Cuddy and Dana Carvey studied the influence of our body language, and the results were mind-boggling. They found out that holding so-called "power postures" for two minutes create a 20 percent increase in testosterone (which boosts confidence) and a 25 percent decrease in cortisol (which reduces stress).

Try it. It actually helps before important presentations, meetings, interviews or competitions. Put your hands on your hips and spread your feet apart (think wonder woman) or lean back in a chair and spread your arms. Hold the posture for at least two minutes...and see what happens!

To learn more about it watch Amy Cuddy's amazing TED Talk called "Your body language shapes who you are."

11 - Turn off your TV

If you want to raise your self-esteem, one huge thing you can do is turning off your TV. Yes. I'm not kidding. It will be absolutely beneficial. TV is one of the biggest energy robbers out there. And the worst is the apparent negativity of the media. It's challenging to build healthy self-esteem, while we mostly see hatred, bloodshed, unhappiness, terrorism, corruption, and fraud on TV. How can you remain positive, hopeful and optimistic in a world like this? Have you ever felt renewed or re-energized after watching TV?

Media is biased towards the negative and the news actually turns us into pessimists by magnifying the negative. We are shown terror when billions of people want to live in peace. We are shown fraud when there are billions of honest transactions going on every day. We are shown that one parent who abuses their child when there are millions of parents loving their children beyond measure. And my friend - it gets even worse (before it will get better) - there is a system to it:

As Dean Graziosi discovers in his book "Millionaire success habits, in the 1950s Time Magazine's covers were about 90% positive. Unfortunately for us editors realized that the more negative their stories would be, the more they would sell - let's not forget that media are companies and WANT and HAVE TO to make profits. So guess what happened when they noticed that negative superlatives work 30% better to get readers attention than positive ones, or that average click-through rates on negative headlines skyrocket and are a whopping 63% higher than that of positive headlines? Exactly. The result is what we see today in the media all over: Negativity.

The problem with that is that if our focus is on the negative all the time if we hear and see this all the time, we'll end up seeing more of it. And then we start to believe that we have to commit fraud to become a CEO, or to be corrupt if we want to be politicians. Why? Because the millions of people who are succeeding honestly are not reported on.

Another problem is that these constant negative feedback can lead to resignation. Why would you start something good if our planet is doomed? Why falling in love if everybody else seems to get a divorce, etc.

Why would you expose yourself to so much negativity? Why not substitute your habit of watching TV for a healthier habit like taking a walk, spending more time with your family, or reading a good book.

Do yourself a favor. Turn off your TV, recover your self-esteem and have some fun in the real world!

12 - Learn to say NO

There might be persons in your life who will try to convince you to do things even if you don't want to do them, and sometimes because we want to please everyone, we say yes to them even if our inner voice cries "NOOOOOO." Saying yes when we mean no hurts our self-esteem and the usual result is that later we feel kind of sad or even angry, because we once again gave in even when we had something better to do.

Learning to say no will improve your life a lot. You will become more of YOU because every time you say YES when you mean NO you lose a little bit of yourself and your self-esteem takes a hit.

When you decide that a "Yes" is a "Yes" and a "No" is a "No," you'll feel much better. This means fewer commitments and although telling your friends and family "NO" is hard at the beginning, the benefits are great eventually.

Don't other people say NO to YOU all the time? You still like them, don't you? Well, you can start saying NO too. It's also a good way to filter out toxic people and fake friends.

While those might make drama, your real friends will understand you and like you even if you tell them NO every now and then. They might even like you more because you become more authentic.

In my work life, the impact of saying NO was even bigger. I improved my work life a lot and actually freed up a lot of time. If you don't say no, you will be the most liked person in the office. You will also be overwhelmed, working extra hours when others go home because you will be doing the work that nobody else wants to do.

The most successful people say "No" very often. Make sure you say "NO" without feeling guilty. You can explain to the person in question that it's nothing personal against them, but for your own well-being. You can still do your colleagues a favor, but only if you have enough time and decide to.

Selfish? Yes! But don't forget who the most important person in your life is. That's right! YOU are the most important person in your life. You have to be well. Only when you are well yourself, can you be well towards others and from this level you can contribute to others. You can always buy some time and say "maybe" at first until you come to a definite decision. Life gets a lot easier if you start saying "No"!

13 - Set boundaries and thrive

Remember that people treat you the way you allow them to treat you. If you want people to treat you differently, you need to raise your standards and set boundaries.

Boundaries are things that people just can't do around you,

like talking down to you, making stupid jokes about you, being disrespectful, yelling at you, being late, interrupting your while you speak, or lying. Communicate your new boundaries clearly and stick with them.

Many people will tell you that they can't recognize you anymore, that you have changed. Those are the manipulators. Don't bother about them. It's because of them you set new boundaries in the first place.

Address anything that bothers you on the spot. That will save you from a lot of headaches and the "shoulda, coulda, woulda." Remember that you can say just anything in the right tone. The art is to find the right tone. You can learn using the right tone by practicing saying things in a neutral tone of voice like you'd say for example "the sky is blue."

If somebody oversteps your boundaries, use the following four-step system. Inform -request - insist - walk away.

For example, if somebody talks down to you, you inform them: "I didn't like that comment" or "I don't like you talking to me in that tone." If they keep on, you request them to stop: "Please stop talking to me like this." Usually, that's when most people back off, but there will always be one or two that continue. With those you have to get a little more serious and insist: "I insist that you stop talking to me this way." If all three steps don't help – leave. Leave the situation. State neutrally, "I can't have this conversation, while you are _____. Let's talk later." and walk away.

Setting boundaries will improve your life and your self-esteem a lot.

Part VII - Be Here, Now

1 - Be happy now

Happiness is a journey, not a destination. Happiness is not something that happens to you from the outside. Happiness is a habit, a state of mind. Happiness is so many things. But the decisive and most important thing is: What is happiness to YOU?

The latest studies have found that happiness is not a thing that happens to you from the outside. It's a choice you make, but it requires effort. The good news is: It can be taught. It's those small habits like gratitude, exercise, meditation, smiling and asking yourself "What can I do to be happier in the present moment."

You can be happy right now! Don't you believe me? Okay. Close your eyes for a moment. Think of a situation that made you really, really happy. Relive this situation in your mind. Feel it, smell it, hear it! Remember the excitement and joy! So? How did it feel? Did it work? How are you feeling now? Happiness doesn't depend on your car, your house, or anything in the outside world. You can be happy right here, right now!

Science has found that your external circumstances make only 10% of your happiness. Surprisingly where you are born, how much you earn, where you live, where you work has a remarkably small impact on your happiness.

50% is genetical. Yes, some people are born happier than others. A whopping 40% of your happiness can be influenced by intentional activities. This is where the gratitude, the long walks, the meditation comes in. This also means if you are born less happy you can improve your happiness by doing these intentional activities.

Don't postpone your happiness to the future, the new apartment, the new car, the promotion. Happiness is right here, right now. In a sunrise, in the smile of your children, in a beautiful piece of music, you are listening to. Sometimes - when you stop chasing happiness and just stand still, you might notice that happiness has been on your heels all along.

Your happiness - same as your self-esteem - depends solely on you. Other people may influence it in specific ways, but ultimately, it's always you who decides, who chooses how happy you want to be.

2 - Be nice

How you treat others is very closely related to how you treat yourself. So, be nice! It will pay you dividends in the long-term.

Emotions are contagious. Scientists have found that if you put three people in a room together, the most emotionally expressive one "infects" the other two with his or her emotions - this works both ways: positive or negative.
Choose to infect others with positive energy. It will only be beneficial, because as they say "what goes around comes around."

You already learned the power of your spoken words. Use your words positively, use them to empower people. Words have such a significant impact. It's scientifically proven that our words can influence the performance of others. They can change the mentality of a person which in turn changes their achievements. For example, when researchers remind older people that memory usually decreases with age, they perform worse on memory tests than those who weren't reminded of that detail.

See the greatness in others. If you can see their greatness, you are actually contributing to that greatness. The Pygmalion Effect teaches us that our belief in the potential of a person awakens this potential. When we believe that our colleagues, friends and family members can do more and achieve more, this is very often the exact reason for why they do. Unfortunately, this also works the other way round - which very often is the case.

Every time you meet someone, try and see the greatness that lies in this person. Ask yourself "What makes them special? What's their gift?" As you focus on it, you will discover it. It also makes you more tolerant of not-so-friendly people. You

can say "I'm sure they have great qualities, and today they only have a bad day..."
Be nice! And let me know how it goes for you.

P.S.: Being nice doesn't mean that you have to let other people fool you, or say yes to everything. Nice people also say no or enough is enough.

3 - Be prepared

A famous saying goes that "luck" is "when preparation meets opportunity." There might be more to it or not, but it surely doesn't cause any harm to be prepared. Learn everything there is to learn about your job, about your industry, about your presentation or about whatever is next on your list. If you are prepared and have the knowledge to back it up, you will feel much more secure, and your self-esteem will go up.

Even if we are super prepared, there's always something that we can't know. Be ready to admit it. You don't have to know everything. My former University professor Angel Miro once told me: "Marc, you don't always have to have all the information, but you have to know where to find it."

Keep working on your personal and professional development. Commit yourself to becoming the best person you can be. Stay hungry! When researchers studied extraordinarily successful people, those had two characteristics in common that separated them from the rest. First of all, they believed in themselves. They believed they could do it and second: They always wanted to learn more. They kept asking questions. They kept on learning.

Stay curious and eager to learn new things and better yourself. The wiser you become, the more valuable you become for your company.

Read books, take a workshop. Today, you can learn the best tricks of management, leadership, time management or financial planning in a two or four-hour workshop that will benefit you for the rest of your life.

I make it a habit to read at least one book a week, buy a new course every two months, and sign up for at least two seminars or workshops a year. What are you going to do?

4 - Be the change

Often, life would be so much better and so much easier if people just changed the way they act and be more like us, right? Or, even better if they would see the world just like us. Oh, yes. That would be nice. It also won't happen. You can't change other people. Period. This is one of the main reasons many of our relationships go downhill. We meet someone, we think "They will change" or even worse "I will change him or her" and after wasting precious time and energy we notice: They didn't change. They will not change just because we want them to, no matter if we cry, constantly complain or even punish them. They will only change if they decide to change. Some might change for a time after our emotional blackmailing succeeds, but usually, they fall back into their old natural behavior relatively quick.

So, the only thing you can do is to lead by example. People usually don't do what you say, but they will do what you do. So, you have to be the change you want to see in others. Eat healthier, exercise, be more polite, be a better spouse, be a better boss, always be punctual, be positive. Be the change you want to see in the world.

You cannot change other people, BUT you can change your attitude towards them. Instead of spending the time to convince them to do what you want them to do, it's a lot quicker and realistic to change your attitude towards them and their actions and behavior. Believe me, once you accept this concept you will erase a lot of small problems from your life.

Remember:
1. Be the change
2. Change your attitude towards the people you want to change

5 - Make a difference - The Power of One

In a world full of problems, wars, scandals, corruption, terrorism, climate change and much more… what can YOU do to make a difference? Is there anything? Yes. I have good news for you. You are more powerful than you think.

We generally underestimate our power to bring change. Yes. One person can really make a significant difference. Why? Because every change begins in the mind of one single person and then it expands. And my friend…It expands exponentially.

We underestimate our capacity to bring change because we underestimate the potential of the exponential function. Think for example about the exponential nature of social networks. It's said that within six degrees of separation we are connected to everyone on this planet.

You are much more powerful than you think. Although there are many things in this world that you can't control, there are also things you can control. You will not stop world pollution, but you can walk, go by bike or public transport or separate your trash. You can choose healthier, non-processed food. If you're not happy with the policy of a certain company, you can stop buying their products. Yes, you are only one. But if a thousand people do the same thing surely someone will notice.

In these rough times, you can decide to be polite to everyone you meet, no matter their color or religion. You can decide to affect the 4 square meters around you positively. What would happen if everybody did this?

You can gift five smiles a day. Smiles are contagious and if everybody that you are smiling at gifts smiles to five other people, in no time the whole world will be smiling :-) The same happens when you compliment people or make people feel good. We are influencing people every minute of our life with our actions and emotions. The only question is: in which direction are we going to do it?

Embrace the power of ONE. It will be very beneficial for your self-esteem.

6 - Forgive everyone

To be a forgiving person is not only good for your self-esteem, but it's also crucial on your journey to success and happiness.

I know. Why forgive someone who did you wrong? Because it's not about being right or wrong, it's about you being well and not wasting energy. Being resentful or angry with people - or even worse - reliving hate and anger over and over again is toxic. It's bad for your energy; it's bad for your health, it's bad for your relationships so, do yourself a favor and forgive. It might be difficult to accept, but you're not doing it for the other person, you are doing it for yourself. Once you forgive and let go, you will sleep better, you will enjoy your present moments more, and a huge weight will be lifted off your shoulders.

They say being angry and having resentments towards another person is like drinking poison and hoping the other individual dies from it. In other words, it's crazy and self-harming. Holding grudges hurts you more than anybody else. The negative feelings that you are feeling will hurt your health and character - and even worse - keeping your focus stuck in the past wounds could attract even more unpleasant experiences into your life.

One thing is clear though. Forgiving others doesn't mean that you are stupid. Or being a forgiving person doesn't mean that people can do to you what they like. Set clear boundaries, put limits on other's behavior, or call them out on the spot. Expel people who hurt you from your life, but don't hold grudges. Let them go, forgive them, forget them and move on. Learn from the experience and be open to new, better experiences to come.

Also - though this might be slightly uncomfortable - call people that you have wronged or hurt, and honestly apologize, or at least write them a letter.

7 - Forgive yourself

If there is any shortcut to a healthy self-esteem, this is probably it. When you manage to forgive yourself, you take your self-esteem to another level. It's all about kindness to ourselves and having compassion - not only for others but for ourselves. (Do not confuse this with self-pity, which is toxic.)

One of the reasons for low self-esteem is because we feel guilty for something we have done or left undone, so it's essential to forgive yourself. Once you've done this, your self-esteem will increase, and you'll also be more capable of forgiving others.

Be forgiving to yourself, accept your mistakes and pledge to not repeat them, forgive yourself for your weaknesses (you are only human and don't have to be perfect) and work on your strengths. Forgive yourself for your sins and don't repeat them if possible.

To have a healthy self-esteem, you have to be your own best friend, accept yourself, and forgive yourself first. Once you've done this, the rest will follow.

The changes you will see when you manage to forgive yourself are absolutely amazing! Sometimes illnesses go away; sometimes self-forgiveness clears the last energy block to let wealth come into your life. Just do it and observe what forgiveness will do for you in your life.

8 - Don't take rejection personally

One of the biggest fears we have is the fear of rejection. How many things don't we even try, because we fear rejection? We don't send the offer. We don't talk to the stranger that smiled to us on the train. We don't ask for the business. We don't send our CV.

The good news is: You can learn to handle rejection. You have to. Every now and then you're going to be rejected. It's inevitable. And it's ok. Imagine how boring life would be if you would never be rejected…

The higher your self-esteem, the lower your fear of rejection, and the lower your fear of rejection the better your self-esteem. Be aware that the fear of rejection might only be a movie playing in your mind and above all don't take rejections personally. Rejection has nothing to do with your intrinsic value as a person.

The fun thing is if you get rejected, nothing has actually happened. If you ask someone out and he or she doesn't want to go out with you, actually nothing has changed. He or she was not going out with you before, and he/she is not going out with you now. If you want to make a sale and the client doesn't want to buy, nothing has actually happened. If you apply for a job and you don't get it. Nothing has actually happened. You didn't have the job before, and now you still don't have it. Being rejected is not the problem. Your inner self-talk after being rejected is the problem: "I'm just not good enough. I knew I'd screw it up. Mother/Father was right. I will never achieve anything in life".

Don't take rejection personally and keep on trying. In the last two years, I was rejected so many times I can't even count it anymore. And it hurt - I won't lie to you. But I kept on trying and with patience and persistence things eventually worked out. I was rejected by dozens of publishers; now I'm writing a book for the best. I was rejected by agents; now I have four. Banks wouldn't loan me money to invest. I went back better prepared and got a much better deal.

If you need to hear a 100 "No" a day, to make five sales, would you do it? The problem is that many people are not up for it. It's a numbers game.

Be prepared for rejection. Deal with it when it comes and keep on hustling. When somebody tells you "No, thanks," you think "NEXT."

9 - Let go of the past

Letting go of the past and learning from past behavior is crucial to developing a healthy self-esteem. Feeling guilty about things you have done, or staying stuck in situations that have already passed is not learning from the past. Every moment you spend in your past is a moment you steal from your present and future. You cannot function in the present, while you live in the past. No mind in the world can cope with two realities at a time.

Don't hang on to your drama by reliving it indefinitely. LET GO OF IT! It's over. Focus on what you want instead. You can't change it anymore. What you can do is live your present with higher awareness, knowing that this is what will shape your future.

Only when you dare to let go of the old, can you be open to new things entering your life. Don't waste your time thinking of things that could or should have happened or that didn't work out as you wanted in the past. It doesn't make sense! Your life reflects whatever you dominantly focus on. If your focus is mostly on your past, on the "coulda, shoulda, woulda," you will be constantly frustrated, anxious and confused in the present. This is far too high of a price to pay.

Learn from your past experiences and move on. That's all you have to do from now on. Easy, isn't it? This means recognizing your mistakes and - to the best of your ability and awareness - not repeating them.

Concentrate on what you want to do well in the future and not what went wrong in the past. You need to let go of the past so that you are free and new things can come into your life. Let go of old baggage, finish unfinished business, and get closure with people. Torturing yourself over what you have done, feeling guilty, ashamed or even unworthy is a pure waste of valuable time and energy. These negative emotions will only prevent you from enjoying the present. Use your memories, but don't allow your memories to use you. Complete the past so that you can be free to enjoy the present.

From now on, adopt the mindset that you will always finish your business. Don't leave anything incomplete in your relationships, work, and all other areas. Forgive yourself and keep moving forward with a positive attitude.

10 - Don't be jealous

Let's talk about a really toxic emotion. An emotion that high self-esteem people don't have…or at least not very often. Jealousy. It's a totally useless emotion. First of all, being jealous or envious of other people's lifestyle, money, looks, or friends has no benefit for you. For example, being jealous of other people's money will not bring that money to you. Being jealous of other people's looks will not make you more handsome.

The constant negative emotions of jealousy and envy will make you feel miserable, and you might "attract" even more misery into your life. Not only do they foster discontent and distress - jealousy, for example, can increase stress hormones in your body. Over time, they lead to resentment and bitterness and cause us to do things we wouldn't normally do.

In the worst case, we can get on a downward spiral that ends up in depression. Psychologically, jealousy and envy are linked to a low self-esteem and insecure people.

So, what can you do to overcome those feelings and - even better - how can you use them positively - for example, as motivation and inspiration? You might not believe it, but I've been jealous and envious of other people for a long period of my life. Yup. Me. When I changed my perspective, I started getting out of it. Here's how I did it:

Become aware when the emotions of jealousy and envy creep into your mind, realize that feeling jealous or envious is a waste of time and then redirect them. Substitute them with positive thoughts and ask yourself "Why do I feel this way now?" For example, you are envious of a colleague's promotion. Instead of getting bitter ask yourself, "What can I do to get a promotion?" Accept that these feelings are there and it's okay to have feelings of envy and jealousy every now and then. It's entirely human. Keep in mind that it is one thing to have these feelings of jealousy and envy while ACTING like a jealous person is a completely different thing. Thoughts of envy don't make you a bad person. It's human. The question is how you choose to behave as a result of it.

Love yourself. My improvement started when I read somewhere that jealousy is a sign of low self-confidence and low self-esteem. So, every time I got jealous, I reminded myself that this is a sign of low self-esteem and that I have to work on it. The more you love yourself, the more comfortable you feel with yourself, the higher your self-esteem, the less jealous and envious you get. Stop comparing. Practice gratitude instead. Count your own blessings instead other people's blessings. Probably, this exercise alone can "cure" you of jealousy and envy - if you practice it for three to four weeks (see chapter "Adopt an attitude of gratitude").

Surround yourself with secure and self-confident people and spend some time with grateful people while staying away from toxic people. Don't hang out with people who only send out bad vibes, who are constantly talking bad about others, and spread jealousy and hate. Start celebrating the fortune and success of others. Whether your co-worker gets a promotion or your best friend has a new partner, or anytime somebody gets something you desire…Be genuinely happy for them. Your friends' or colleagues' success doesn't mean that you are failing.

11 - Pay attention and enjoy your life as it happens

It's very important to enjoy the present moment. If you don't, then life passes by, and you won't even notice it, because you are never right here, in the present moment.

When you're working you think of the weekend. On the weekend, you think of all the things you have to do on Monday. When you're eating the appetizer, you think of dessert, and when you are eating dessert, you think of the appetizer. The result is that you never get to fully enjoy neither the one nor the other.

Living like this, you never get to enjoy your point of power, the only moment that counts - the present moment. Eckart Tolle wrote an entire book about "The power of NOW" which I highly recommend to you.

Think about it: Do you have any problem RIGHT NOW just being in the moment?

No, you don't. You have a problem when you think of the past, or when you think of the future. You might have a problem in one minute when you start thinking and worrying again, but right now at this moment, you don't have any problems.

Do you constantly live with guilt for your past actions and with fear of an unknown future? Many people are constantly worrying about things in the past that they can't change, or things in the future that – even funnier - mostly never happen. Meanwhile, they are missing out on the NOW, and all you ever have is now. Be present and enjoy the journey. If most of your present moments are good, your future will automatically be brilliant.

12 - You are not what happened to you in your past

No matter what happened in your past, you are not your past.

No matter what people - or yourself - might be telling you…
…You are not your past habits.
…You are not your past failures.
…You are not how others have treated you.

You are who you think you are right now, at this moment
You are what you do right now, at this moment

No matter what happened in your past. Your future is a clean sheet. Right now, you can make decisions to live your life one way, or the other. Right now you can decide in which direction to move. Will you go the easy way? The way of the victim, blaming everybody else for what's happening in your life? Or will you take your life into your own hands, take the road less traveled, adopt a positive attitude and make the best of everything that happens to you in your life?

You can reinvent yourself right now. Every day brings with it the opportunity to start a new life. The great thing is that you get to choose your identity at each and every moment. Who are you going to be? What are you going to do? It's up to you to decide who you are going to be from this day on.

You are the writer, director and main actor of your story. So, if you don't like how the story is playing out...change it! Your decisions and your attitude make your life.

If you DO some of the things suggested in this book, create new habits, and do just some of the many exercises that you will find here constantly, things will start to shift. It's not going to be easy, and you will need discipline, patience, and persistence. But the results will come.

13 - Give up dwelling on the past or worrying about the future

This quote of Dalai Lama says all you need to know about worrying. Read closely what he says. "If a problem is fixable, if a situation is such that you can do something about it, then there is no need to worry. If it's not fixable, then there is no help in worrying. There is no benefit in worrying whatsoever."

Most of us worry constantly. Either about things that happened in the past that we can't fix, or things in the future that we don't even know if they will ever happen, or about things we have no control over, like the economy, wars, and politics.

I don't know about you, but in my life, most of the things I worried about never happened. The things that happened were far less catastrophic than I imagined, and the really bad stuff - the death of loved ones, accidents, illness - always came unexpected and when I least worried about it.

You will not be able to change the past or the future no matter how much you worry, neither does worrying make things better, right? Sometimes, it actually makes things worse, and the worst is that while worrying you lose the preciousness of the present moment.

Here's a little exercise: Take a pen and paper. Right now. Ready?
Write down all your worries. All of them. Do you have a long list?

Now, erase all the worries that are related to the past and past actions and can't be fixed or changed.

Next, erase all the worries about the future that will probably never happen.

Third, erase all the worries that are outside of your control.

Also, erase worries that are related to other people's opinions that you don't even care about.
Ok. Look at your list now. Everything not erased are things or tasks that need your attention. How much of your long list is left? From experience, I'd say max. 10%.

That means the other 90% are things you can't do anything about and you might as well drop them because all they do is take space in your brain and drain you of your energy.

How would it feel if you eliminated this 90 %?

14 - Show everyone kindness and respect

Remember that every person you meet on your life journey has a story. Probably they have gone through something that has forced them to grow and changed them. Don't forget that every person you meet on the street probably has a story as compelling and complicated as your own. Everybody you meet is as extraordinary as you are - even if it doesn't seem like it at first sight.

The least you can do is to give them a chance. Give them a chance to become a part of your life or to interact without judging and discarding them right away. Everybody has something to offer.

Some of my best friends are people that when I first met them I thought "What a strange person" or "He doesn't seem to be very bright". If I would have guided myself by these superficial judgments I would have lost great friendships. When I look back at my life, I notice that the greatest experiences in my life came from giving people a chance, even if my first impression advised me against it.

Of course, many times, my first impression was also right, and I ended up disappointed. That's a price I'm willing to pay for the good experiences that come from giving people a chance. If they live up to that chance, great! If not, it's their problem.

Treat everyone with kindness and respect. Everyone deserves it, even the ones that are rude to you. The rude ones and the angry ones are probably the ones that need your kindness most. If people are rude to you, it's their problem, not yours. Be nice. If you treat everybody with patience and respect, they will notice your kindness and what goes around comes around. If you are nice, you will attract nice people into your life in the long-term

One good trick is that if somebody is rude, you get nicer and nicer, and the ruder they get, the nicer you get. It works in 99% of the cases, as you will end up winning their sympathy. They are not used to this because they usually feed on people who get defensive and angry with them.

Be nice. It's worth it. Being nice to people is great for your self-esteem because you will think: "I'm treating people nice, I must be a nice person." And then because "Self-concept is destiny" your self-esteem will rise.

BONUS CHAPTER taken from 30 DAYS – The Most Important Hour.

The most important hour of your day is composed of the thirty minutes after you wake up and the thirty minutes before you fall asleep. This is when your subconscious is very receptive. It's of great importance what you do at this time. This hour is crucial for your self-esteem and your success.

The way you start your day will have a huge impact on how the rest of your day develops. I'm sure you have had days which have started off on the wrong foot and from then on it got worse and worse – or the opposite where you woke up feeling that everything will go your way and then it did. That's why it's essential to begin your day well. Most of us just get into a rush from the first minute after waking up, and that's how our days unfold. No wonder most people run around stressed nowadays. What would getting up 30 minutes or an hour earlier every morning do for you?

What if instead of hurrying and gulping down your breakfast or even having it on the way to work, you get up and take half an hour for yourself? Maybe you even create a little morning ritual with a 10 or 15-minute meditation. Do you see what this could do for your life if you made it a habit? Here are some activities for the morning ritual. Give it a shot!

Think positive: Today is going to be a great day!
Remember for 5 minutes what you are grateful for.

15 minutes of quiet time.
Imagine the day that is about to start going very well.
Watch a sunrise.
Go running or take a walk.
Write in your journal.

The last half an hour of your day holds the same importance. The things you do in the last half an hour before sleeping will remain in your subconscious during your sleep. So then, it's time to do the following:

Write into your journal again.
Now is the time for reflecting on your day. What did you do great? What could you have done even better?
Plan your day ahead. What are the most important things you want to get done tomorrow?
Make a to-do list for the next day.
Visualize your ideal day.
Read some inspirational blogs, articles, or chapters of a book.
Listen to music that inspires you.

I highly recommend that you NOT WATCH THE NEWS or MOVIES as this might agitate you before you go to sleep. This is because when you are falling asleep, you are highly receptive to suggestions. That's why it's a lot more beneficial to listen or watch positive material.

The planning ahead of your day and the list of things to do can bring you immense advantages and time-saving. The things you have to do will already be in your subconscious plus you will get to work very focused the next day if you already know what your priorities are.

Epilogue

Millions of people all over the world suffer from low self-esteem. You're not alone.

I hope this book has helped you to understand that you are enough!

Know you can do it, know what you are good at, and know you can make it happen.

Love yourself like you love your neighbors and your friends and be extremely nice to yourself.

Do the exercises of this little book that work best for you and repeat them often.

Having high levels of self-esteem and self-confidence will help you deal with any situation and take the best action. You'll be better able to deal with unexpected and undesirable events. Your personal relationships will improve as you will communicate better and you will know that sometimes it's better not to be right, but at peace.

Your better self-esteem will result in you being more successful, having better relationships and you will even be healthier.

I hope that by now you are freed from other people's criticism and judgments and can better express you your thoughts, feelings, values, and opinions.
You have learned that your self-worth doesn't come from the outside - from the acceptance of others - but from the inside.

And that is something you are in control of. With the falling away of self-doubts and self-torturing, you can concentrate on your strengths and will experience more happiness and enjoyment in all areas of your life.

It has been an honor to accompany you on your journey. Now go practice, practice, practice and boost your self-esteem.

Have fun!

I'd be happy to hear about your progress. You can send me an email to
marc@marcreklau.com

I Need Your Help.

Thank You Very Much For Downloading My Book!

I really appreciate your feedback, and love hearing what you have to say. Your input is important for me to make my next book(s) even better.

If you liked the book please be so kind and leave an honest review on Amazon!

It really helps other people to find the book! Five stars would be great though ;-)

Thank you so much!!

Marc

Bring the simple steps of 30 DAYS to your Organization

Help each member of your organization to succeed. My international bestselling book *30 DAYS - change your habits change your life* is available at a special price on bulk orders for businesses, universities, schools, governments, NGOs, and community groups.

It's the ideal gift to inspire your friends, colleagues and team members to reach their fullest potential and make real, sustainable changes.

Contact marc@marcreklau.com

To book a presentation based on 30 DAYS or my latest book Destination Happiness contact me with an e-mail to marc@marcreklau.com

About the Author

Marc Reklau is a Coach, Speaker, and author of 7 books including the #1 Amazon Bestseller "30 Days - Change your habits, change your life", which since April 2015 has been sold and downloaded over 180,000 times and has been translated into Spanish, German, Japanese, Thai, Indonesian, Portuguese and Korean.

He wrote the book in 2014 after being fired from his job and literally went from jobless to Bestseller (which is actually the title of his second book).

The Spanish version of his latest book "Destination Happiness" has been published by Spain's #1 Publisher Planeta in January 2018.

Marc's mission is to empower people to create the life they want and to give them the resources and tools to make it happen.

His message is simple: Many people want to change things in their lives, but few are willing to do a simple set of exercises constantly over a period of time. You can plan and create success and happiness in your life by installing habits that support you on the way to your goals.

If you want to work with Marc directly contact him on his homepage www.marcreklau.com where you also find more information about him.

You can connect with him on Twitter @MarcReklau, Facebook or on his website www.goodhabitsacademy.com

Marc's other books

30 Days - Change your habits, change your life
Contains the best strategies to help you to create the life you want. The book is based on science, neuroscience, positive psychology and real-life examples and contains the best exercises to quickly create momentum towards a happier, healthier and wealthier life.
Thirty days can really make a difference if you do things consistently and develop new habits!

More than 180000 combined sales and downloads since March 2015.

From Jobless to Amazon Bestseller
From Jobless to Amazon Bestseller shows you the simple, step-by-step system that author Marc Reklau used to write, self publish, market and promote his book to over 130,000 combined sales and downloads on Amazon.

The Productivity Revolution
What if you could dramatically increase your productivity? What if you could stop being overwhelmed and get an extra hour a day to do the things you love? What would finally having time to spend with your family, some alone time to read, or exercise mean to you?
Learn the best strategies to double your productivity and get things done in this book.

More than 10000 copies sold!

Destination Happiness
In his newest book, bestselling author, Marc Reklau, shows you **scientifically proven exercises and habits** that help you to achieve a successful, meaningful and happy life. Science has proven that Happiness and Optimism can be learned. Learn the best and scientifically proven methods to improve your life now and don't be fooled by the simplicity of some of the exercises!

One last thing...

If you have been inspired by my books and want to help others to reach their goals and improve their lives, here are some action steps you can take immediately to make a positive difference:

Gift my books to friends, family, colleagues and even strangers so that they can also learn that they can reach their goals and live great lives.

Please share your thoughts about this book on Twitter, Facebook and Instagram or write a book review. It helps other people to find 30 DAYS.

If you own a business or if you are a manager - or even if you're not - gift some copies to your team or employees and improve the productivity of your company. Contact me at marc@marcreklau.com. I'll give you a 30% discount on bulk orders.

If you have a Podcast or know somebody that has one ask them to interview me. I'm always happy to spread the message of 30 DAYS and help people improve their lives. You can also ask you local newspaper, radio station, or online media outlets to interview me :)